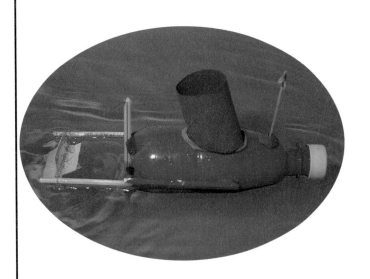

This edition produced in **1993** for
Shooting Star Press Inc
230 Fifth Avenue
New York, NY 10001

© Aladdin Books Ltd 1993

Created and produced by
NW Books
28 Percy Street
London W1P 9FF

ISBN 1-56924-043-4

Material originally produced in
the Science Workshop series.
Published in the
United States in 1992 by
Gloucester Press
95 Madison Avenue
New York, NY 10016

CONTENTS

Design	David West
	Children's Book Design
Editors	Suzanne Melia
	Catherine Warren
	Michael Flaherty
Designer	Stephen Woosnam-Savage
Picture Researcher	Emma Krikler
Illustrators	Ian Thompson
	Ian Moores
Consultants	Caroline Pontefract
	Geoff Leyland
	Bryson Gore

science WORKSHOP

Pam Robson
Mick Seller

SHOOTING STAR PRESS

THE WORKSHOP

A science workshop is a place to test ideas, perform experiments, and make discoveries. To prove many scientific facts you don't need a lot of fancy equipment. In fact, everything you need for a basic workshop can be found around your home or school. Read through these pages, and then use your imagination to add to your "home laboratory." Make sure that you are aware of the relevant safety rules, and take care of the environment. A science experiment is an activity that involves the use of basic rules to test a hypothesis. A qualitative approach involves observation. A quantitative approach involves measurement. Remember, one of the keys to being a creative scientist is to keep experimenting. This means experimenting with equipment to give you the most accurate results as well as experimenting with ideas. In this way you will build up your workshop as you go along.

MAKING THE MODELS

Before you begin, read through all the steps. Then make a list of the things you need and gather them together. Next, think about the project so that you have a clear idea of what you are about to do. Finally, take your time in putting the pieces together. You will find that your projects work best if you wait while glue or paint dries. If something goes wrong, retrace your steps. And, if you can't fix it, start over again. Every scientist makes mistakes, but the best ones know when to begin again!

GENERAL TIPS

There are at least two parts to every experiment: experimenting with materials and testing a science "fact." If you don't have all the materials, experiment with others instead. For example, if you can't find any polystyrene (a hard plastic), use cardboard or balsa wood instead. Once you've finished experimenting, read your notes thoroughly and think about what happened, evaluating your measurements and observations. See what conclusions you can draw from your results.

SAFETY WARNINGS

Make sure that an adult knows what you are doing at all times. Cutting and bending a coat hanger can be dangerous. Ask an adult to do this for you. In the experiments that use electricity, always use a battery of 1.5 volts. Always make sure your hands are dry. Water and electricity do not mix. Never use main-line electricity. Always be careful with scissors. If you spill any water, wipe it up right away. Slippery surfaces are dangerous. Clean up your workshop when you finish!

EXPERIMENTING

Always conduct a "fair test." This means changing one thing at a time for each stage of an experiment. In this way you can always tell which change caused a different result. As you go along, record what you see and compare it to what you thought would happen. Ask questions such as "why?" "how?" and "what if ?" Then test your model and write down the answers.

AIR, WIND AND FLIGHT

INTRODUCTION

Air is all around us. Even though we cannot see it, taste it, or grab hold of it, air is essential to life on Earth. Invisible air is not empty space. It is actually a rich mix of many different gases, including the oxygen that we breathe. The blanket of air surrounding our planet is thick and heavy. Indeed, the force of air pressure pushes on us from every direction. We can measure slight air changes in this pressure to forecast the weather. Movements of hot and cold air, which make nature's gentle breezes and fierce hurricanes, can be utilized to launch a hot-air balloon. Changes in air pressure, made by the delicate curve of a wing, make flight possible, while the force of air resistance, captured with a parachute, cushions a landing. The power of wind can be trapped by windmills to drive machines, and sails to propel boats. The gases in the atmosphere can be compressed to fit into a smaller volume. This allows large amounts of air to be stored, for example, in small metal cylinders such as the aqualungs used by divers to breathe underwater. Plentiful and fascinating, air promises science and technology new discoveries for centuries to come.

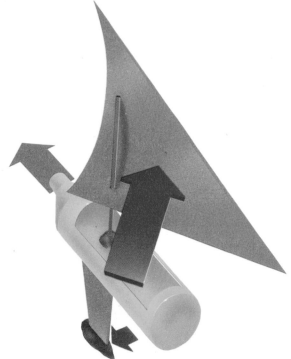

ESSENTIAL OXYGEN

Everything around us is either solid, a liquid, or a gas. Gases are the lightest (or least dense) of all. Solid things, like cars, can move through gases. The air around us is a mixture of gases. Most of the air, about four-fifths, is nitrogen. About one-fifth is oxygen. Then there are small amounts of other gases, argon, helium, krypton, xenon, neon, and carbon dioxide. Finally, there is some water vapor in the air. Without oxygen we could not breathe, and without oxygen fires would not burn – like us they would suffocate. In about 1670 the English doctor John Mayow proved that fire consumes air. By repeating his experiment, you can also see how a flame uses up a part of the air.

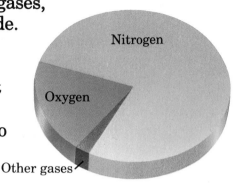

Nitrogen

Oxygen

Other gases

"BREATHING" FIRE

1 To test that fire actually burns air, you need a few household items. Find a bowl made of something that is fireproof (not plastic), three coins, a clean glass jar, modeling clay, and a candle.

2 Push a small lump of clay onto the middle of the bowl. Arrange the coins so that the top of the jar will rest on them without wobbling. Firmly push the candle into the clay and half fill the bowl with water.

3 Ask an adult to help you with this step. Light the candle and then very carefully lower the glass jar over the flame, resting it on the coins. Quickly mark the water level on the side of the jar. Watch the flame closely to see how it changes.

1

2

3

WHY IT WORKS

The flame uses up the oxygen in the air as it burns. Once much of the oxygen is taken up, there is no longer enough to support a flame and the candle goes out. Air pressure (see pages 10, 11) pushes on the water outside the jar. Inside the jar, the water is forced into the space left by the oxygen. The water level inside rises by about one-fifth, the fraction of oxygen in the air.

This experiment is not exact. Some of the air escapes from the jar as the flame burns because air expands when heated. As the air cools down it shrinks, or contracts, making extra space for the water to fill.

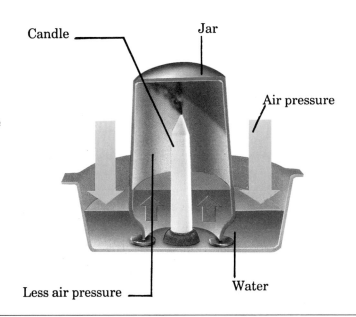

Candle

Jar

Air pressure

Less air pressure

Water

4 Note what happens to the water at the bottom of the bowl. As the candle burns notice if bubbles appear. When the candle goes out see if the water level rises inside the jar. Observe how high it has risen. Mark the side of the glass to show the new water level.

4

BRIGHT IDEAS

Light two candles. Cover one with a small jar and one with a large jar. See which candle burns the longest.

Place a dried pea into the neck of a bottle. Blow hard to make the pea go into the bottle. Notice whether the air pressure inside the bottle is strong enough to keep the pea out.

POWERFUL PRESSURE

Although we don't really notice it much, the air is all around us and is pressing on us all the time. Air pressure is caused because air has weight and it is pulled down to Earth by gravity. As it is pulled down it squeezes against things – this is air pressure. Our own blood pressure presses back against the air – if we suddenly took air pressure away, our bodies would explode. This is why spacemen have to wear special pressurized suits: in space there is no air and so no air pressure. Slight changes in air pressure give us a clue about weather changes. We can measure air pressure and so predict the weather with an instrument called a barometer.

WEATHER FORECASTING

1 You can make a simple barometer by using a new balloon, a clean glass jar, a straw, a toothpick, a rubber band, oak tag, and some cardboard. Cut the neck off the balloon. Stretch the balloon over the jar. Hold it in place with the rubber band.

1

2

2 Tape the toothpick to the end of the straw. Tape the other end of the straw to the center of the balloon lid. Make a weather picture chart on the oak tag, with the good weather at the top.

3

3 Fold the sheet of oak tag and cut a cardboard triangle for a support. Fix the weather chart in position. Put the barometer in place and watch the pointer move a little each day.

WHY IT WORKS

Air pressure changes all the time. It pushes on us from all directions because of the endless jostling of gas molecules. When the air pressure rises, indicating good weather, the pressure pushes down on your barometer's lid, making the straw pointer rise. When the air pressure drops, indicating bad weather, the lid swells and the pointer drops. Air temperature also affects pressure. Your barometer is most accurate when kept at a steady temperature.

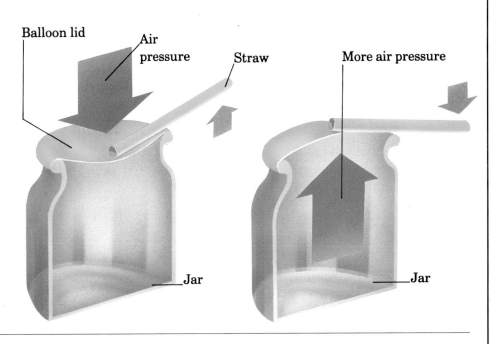

Balloon lid Air pressure Straw More air pressure Jar Jar

BRIGHT IDEAS

Try to lift a piece of paper from a tabletop using only a ruler as in the picture. Feel the air pressure try to stop you.

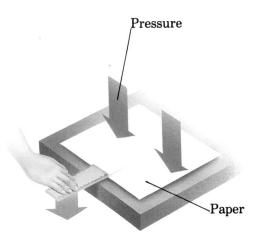

Pressure Paper

Very carefully hang a ruler from its center by a string so that it balances perfectly. Take two identical balloons and blow one up. Tape the balloons to either end of the ruler. You'll need identical pieces of tape to keep the experiment fair. Notice what happens. Which balloon is the heaviest and why?

Empty balloon

Full balloon

RISING CURRENTS

Have you ever wondered what makes the wind blow? As the air is warmed by the Sun it expands and becomes lighter. These changes cause the warm air to rise. At the same time, cooler air moves in, filling up the space left behind. So, the air is moving, and moving air is wind. The rotation of the Earth complicates the pattern, causing wind to swirl. Satellite images of the Earth show the clouds above us in constant motion due to these air currents.

MOBILE AIR

1

1 You can prove that hot air rises with a mobile that spins in the slightest current. Cut some shapes from aluminum foil. For the mobile shown here you need two squares and two circles.

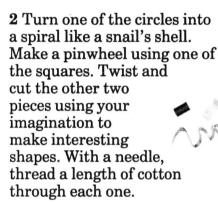

2 Turn one of the circles into a spiral like a snail's shell. Make a pinwheel using one of the squares. Twist and cut the other two pieces using your imagination to make interesting shapes. With a needle, thread a length of cotton through each one.

2

3

3 Cut a triangle from a piece of cardboard. Decorate one side and tape a stick securely to the other to make the stand. Attach a piece of clay to the bottom of the stick. Make sure the complete stand balances upright evenly.

4

4 Carefully tape the thread lengths to the back of the triangle. Make sure each shape can twist freely. Place your mobile above a radiator, keeping it well away from gas and fire and breezes. Watch the shapes twirl.

BRIGHT IDEAS

The spirals turn very nicely in the currents of rising hot air, but would other shapes turn as well? Try a twisted loop, a circle, a strip. Notice which works best. Are the best shapes similar to birds' feathers or the wings of a glider? Do the spirals work better with longer or shorter strings? Is close to the radiator best, or high above it?

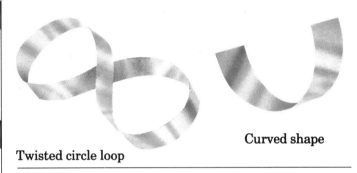

Twisted circle loop

Curved shape

WHY IT WORKS

Although dangling at rest when placed elsewhere in a room, your mobile shapes twirl when hung above a radiator. This is because rising warm air pushes upward on the edges of the shapes, causing them to twist and turn like a propeller.

The movements of hot and cold air are called convection currents and cause many winds. The hottest part of the Earth is the equator – here the air is heated and it rises. High in the air it travels out toward the poles. At the cold North and South poles the air cools and falls, then travels toward the equator.

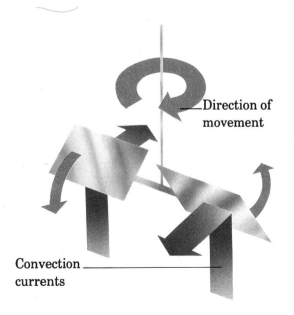

Direction of movement

Convection currents

CAPTURING WIND

More than four thousand years ago people were already capturing the wind in sails to move boats through the water. These boats had "square rigged" sails which caught the wind, and oars for rowing when the wind blew the wrong way or when there was no wind at all. About 1,500 years ago, sailors discovered that with a special triangular sail called a "lateen" they could actually sail against the wind. Modern sailboats have tough, nylon sails designed to catch the wind from any angle. A windsurfer's single sail swivels around the board to take the craft in any direction. By trying it out on a simple boat, we can see how a lateen sail works.

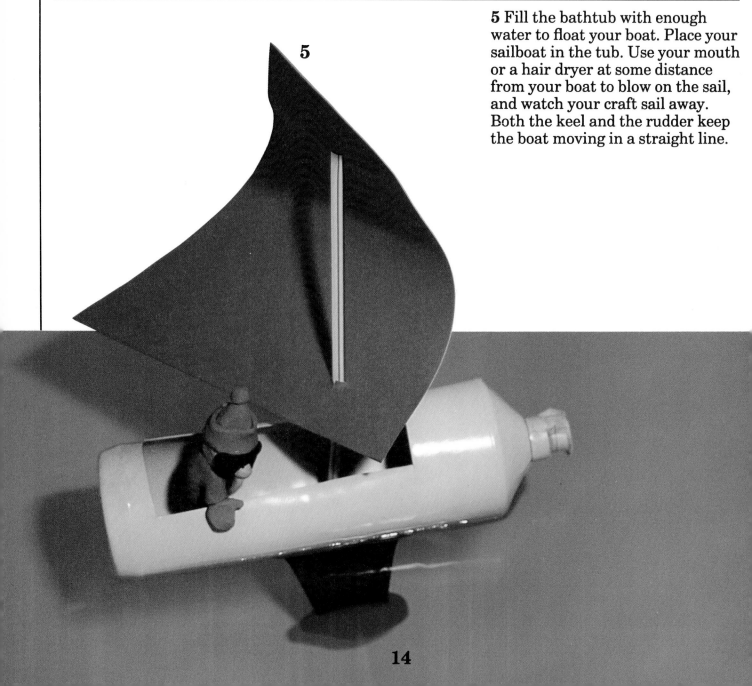

5 Fill the bathtub with enough water to float your boat. Place your sailboat in the tub. Use your mouth or a hair dryer at some distance from your boat to blow on the sail, and watch your craft sail away. Both the keel and the rudder keep the boat moving in a straight line.

5

SAIL POWER

1 To make a sailboat, first cut a rectangular hole in the side of a plastic bottle.

1

2 Secure a blob of modeling clay inside the bottle boat. Use it to hold your straw mast in place.

2

3 Cut a triangle from a piece of paper and decorate it if you wish. Pierce two holes through your sail. Feed the mast through the holes.

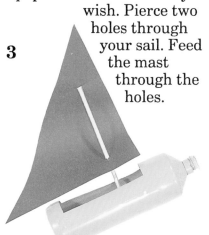

3

4 Cut a wedge shape from a juice carton for your waterproof keel. Put a chunk of clay on each end and attach it to the boat.

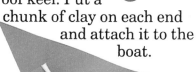

4

WHY IT WORKS

No matter which way you blow on it, your sailboat can be made to go in any direction. When the wind is directly behind the boat, holding the sail at right angles to the wind channels your boat forward. You can move at right angles, or "across" the wind by again fixing the sail at right angles to the breeze. The boat pictured here is sailing across the wind.

For a "square rigged" boat, the sail is caught in the currents of moving air and pushed along – a bit like you blowing a Ping Pong ball across a table. For a triangular sail the effect is different. The wind blows over the top of the sail and causes low pressure which sucks the sail, and the boat, forward.

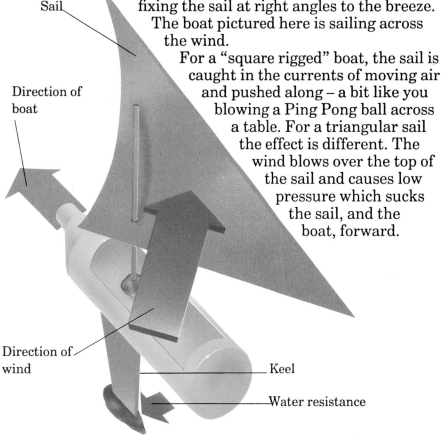

Sail

Direction of boat

Direction of wind

Keel

Water resistance

BRIGHT IDEAS

Which shape do you think is the best for a sail? Experiment with squares, rectangles, circles, and triangles. Once you've found the best shape, try it out in different sizes. Find out if a smaller sail or a larger sail is the best one.

Try blowing on your boat from different directions. Watch how the boat moves every time. Now, keeping the "wind" blowing from one direction, see what happens when the sail is fixed as pictured in the two ways below.

Sail fixed at front of boat

Sail fixed at rear of boat

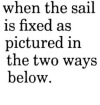

Pressure Changes

Even though the rush of wind blows things about, moving air has lower pressure than still air. This is because air molecules have a set amount of energy. When air flows slowly, it has energy left to create sizable pressure. But when air moves quickly, this motion takes up a lot of energy. Therefore, less energy goes into making pressure and the air pressure drops. Because of this, when air moves between things, the air pressure between them is low and the higher surrounding pressure will push them together. Even the tops of tall buildings bow together a little bit on a windy day. This can be illustrated in the project below using simple materials to simulate skyscrapers on a windy day.

Blowing Balls

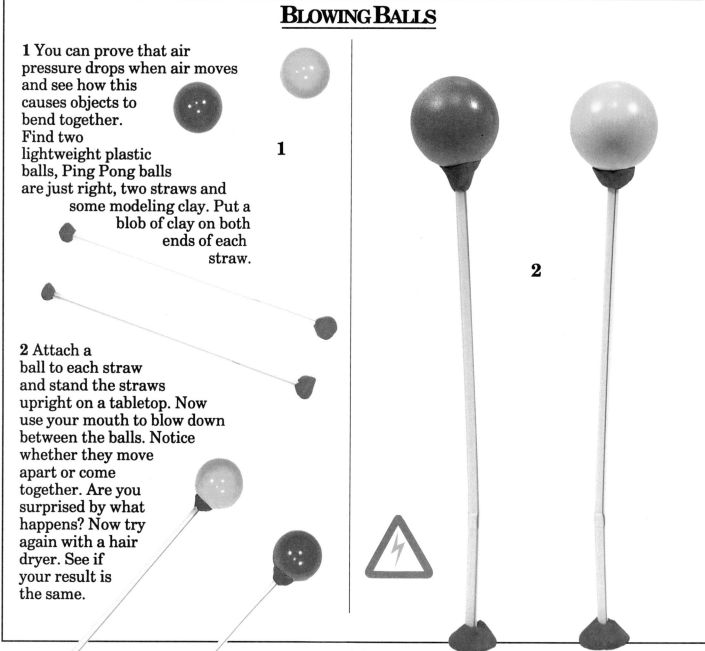

1 You can prove that air pressure drops when air moves and see how this causes objects to bend together. Find two lightweight plastic balls, Ping Pong balls are just right, two straws and some modeling clay. Put a blob of clay on both ends of each straw.

1

2

2 Attach a ball to each straw and stand the straws upright on a tabletop. Now use your mouth to blow down between the balls. Notice whether they move apart or come together. Are you surprised by what happens? Now try again with a hair dryer. See if your result is the same.

Bright Ideas

☀ Try blowing the air onto the standing Ping Pong balls from different directions. See if the balls are still drawn together when the air hits them from the side or from below.

☀ Hold two strips of paper about 2 inches apart and blow between them. See how the fast moving air pulls the strips inward.

☀ Hold a strip of paper loosely in front of your mouth and blow over the top. Does the paper rise?

☀ Cut two small flaps in the end of the strip. Bend one flap down. Blow over the paper again. Notice how the flaps change the paper's motion. Rest a piece of paper over a gap between two books. Blow underneath the paper and watch where it goes.

☀ Place a small cardboard disk on a table and see if you can lift it simply by blowing over the top.

Why It Works

When you direct fast moving air between the balls they come together. This is known as the "Bernoulli effect," named after the Swiss mathematician David Bernoulli. More than 250 years ago, he discovered that when water is forced through a constriction in a pipe, its speed increases, but its pressure drops.

Fast moving air has low pressure, too. As you squeeze fast moving air past the two balls it makes a low pressure pocket between them. The "high pressure" air on either side of the balls pushes them into this pocket, thrusting them together.

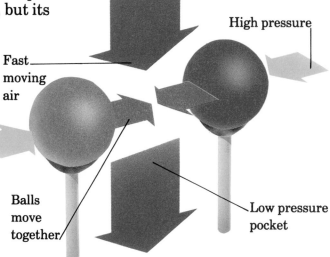

Fast moving air

High pressure

Balls move together

Low pressure pocket

AIR RESISTANCE

If you open an umbrella and try to run with it on a calm day, you will find it difficult as the umbrella captures the air like a parachute, dragging you back. Whenever we move we have to push the air out of the way and we experience air resistance. Sometimes air resistance is helpful, for example in slowing down a parachute. It becomes a nuisance when it acts against a sports car. Some shapes are "streamlined" to move smoothly through the air. They experience less air resistance because the air does not rub against them too much and block their movement.

STREAMLINED SHAPES

1 You can test the force of air resistance. To make a fair test you need two of the same model cars. Make sure their wheels turn freely.

2 Cut two rectangles from a piece of cardboard. Again, to keep the test fair, make them the same size and shape.

3 Attach the rectangular cardboard to the front end of each car. Fold one smoothly over the top and bend the other one as shown. Tape them in place.

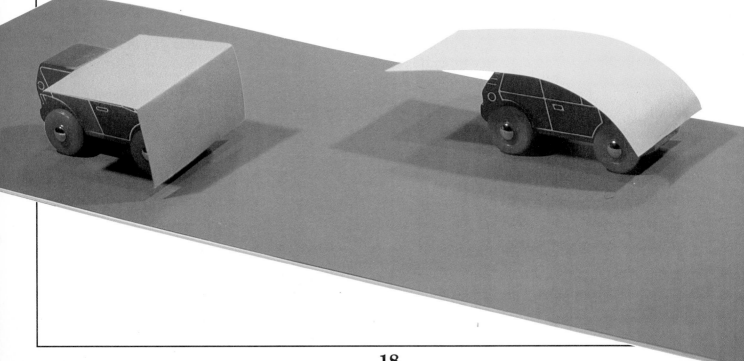

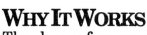

WHY IT WORKS

The shape of your cars makes them roll quickly or slowly. Air flows smoothly over the car with the rounded paper front. This streamlining allows it to roll faster than the car with the square front, which is held back by air resistance, or drag. Drag slows things down, creating ripples of air behind them. These moving ripples, or eddies, lower the air pressure behind the unstreamlined car, keeping it back as it moves.

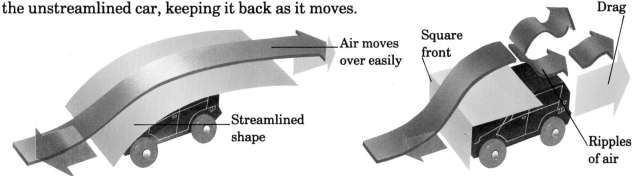

Air moves over easily

Streamlined shape

Square front

Drag

Ripples of air

4 Tilt a board on a book to form a ramp. Release the cars at the same time from the top of the ramp into a wind from a hair dryer. Notice which one experiences least air resistance.

BRIGHT IDEAS

Capture air with a simple parachute. Tie four strings to the corners of a large handkerchief. Fix a blob of modeling clay to the strings. Now make a larger parachute from paper, attaching the same piece of clay. It will drop more slowly than the first one because it captures more air.

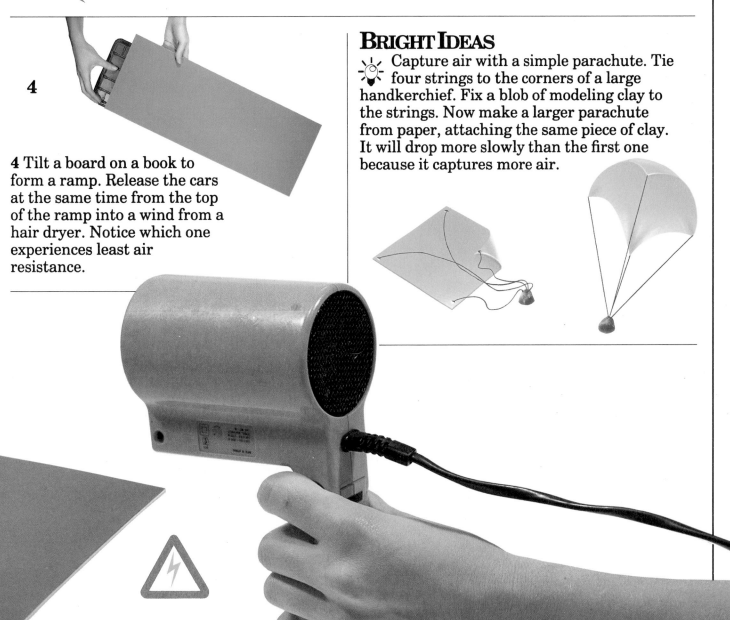

WINGS IN FLIGHT

Birds, insects, bats, and airplanes all need wings to fly. When the Wright brothers made the first powered flight in 1903, it was after years of studying nature's wings. Whether wings are made of something as light as feather or as rigid as metal, it is their shape that gives them lift. This special wing shape is known as an airfoil. Flat on the bottom and curved on top, the airfoil cuts through the air, creating low pressure above which helps the airfoil to rise. You can demonstrate this in the project below.

AIRFOIL

1 To make your own flying wing you need a piece of oak tag measuring about 4in by 6in. Fold the oak tag in two, leaving an overlap of about ½in.

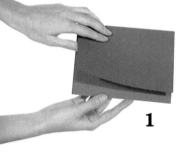

1

2 Push the overlapping ends together. This will make one side of the folded paper curve up. Tape it in place.

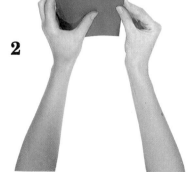

2

3 Use a pen to pierce holes through the wing (top and bottom) as shown.

3

4

4 Carefully push a drinking straw through each set of holes.

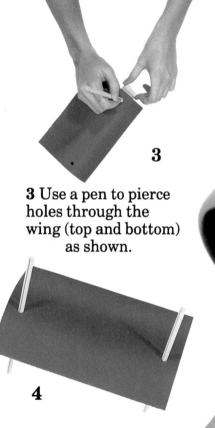

5

5 Pull a long piece of thread through each straw. Pull these tracks tight and fix them straight between a floor and table, so the wing can slide up and down freely. Lift the wing up a little and aim a hair dryer at the folded edge. Turn the dryer on, and watch your wing soar. Make sure you are pointing the dryer straight for the best lift.

BRIGHT IDEAS

Turn your airfoil upside down and test it again. Notice what happens now. Move the hair dryer back from your airfoil. Does it stay up? See how far back you can move the hair dryer before the airfoil drops down.

Make another airfoil double the size. It creates lower pressure above. Try to move the hair dryer even further away.

Larger airfoil

First airfoil

WHY IT WORKS

Your airfoil rises because of its shape. The top surface of the wing is longer than the bottom surface. Air passing over the top of the wing has farther to travel – so it has to go faster. Faster moving air has lower pressure. (Remember the Bernoulli effect!) Low pressure above the wing causes it to lift.

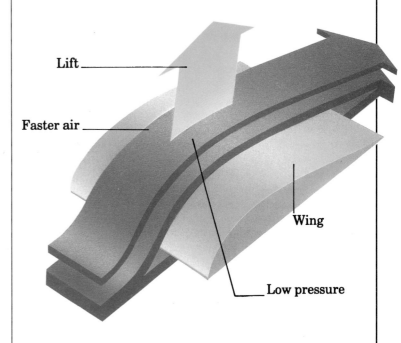

Lift

Faster air

Wing

Low pressure

AIRSTREAM EVIDENCE

Some things are shaped to move through the air very smoothly, such as rockets, airplanes, and racing cars. Can you think of any more?

Designers use a wind tunnel to test streamlined shapes. Streams of smoke are blown over new models to show how air currents move around them. The flow of smoke tells designers how much air resistance their vehicles will have to face. The straighter the flow of smoke – the less it curls when it hits a surface – the more streamlined the shape is and the better it will move through the air.

Fast moving shapes are also slowed down by drag. The faster a car or an aircraft moves, the more that drag holds it back. A low drag shape in a wind tunnel will have straight smoke streams behind it.

You can use a hair dryer and ribbon instead of smoke to study how streamlined different shapes are.

WIND TUNNEL

1 Make a backdrop for watching airstreams.

2 Cut slits in the side of a cereal box for the backdrop. Push two cardboard triangles through the slits.

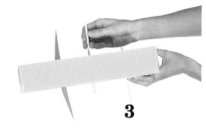

3

3 Carefully make holes through the center of the box and push two thin sticks through them. (These sticks will support shapes for testing, such as your airfoil and a ball.)

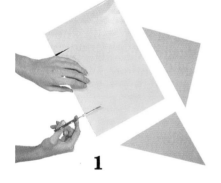

1

2

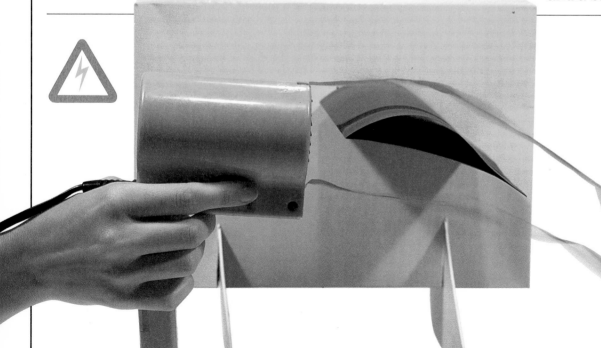

WHY IT WORKS

Your airfoil does not disrupt the lines of smoke – or the ribbons – as they pass over its surface. Instead, the smoke streams continue in almost the same lines as before they struck the wing. This means that the wing can move freely through the air. Air does not rub against it too much, slowing it down by air resistance. (Like water in a simming pool that seems to push us back if we walk through it, air resistance is a powerful force.)

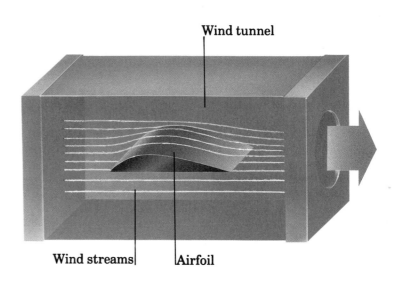

Wind tunnel

Wind streams Airfoil

4 Tape two thin ribbons onto a hair dryer. With the dryer set on "cool," watch how the ribbons blow over your shapes to see the airstreams around them.

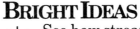

4

BRIGHT IDEAS

See how streams of air move around two different cars. Attach paper fronts to toy cars as shown below (see pages 18, 19). Stand each above a tabletop on a stick of modeling clay. Test each for streamlining.

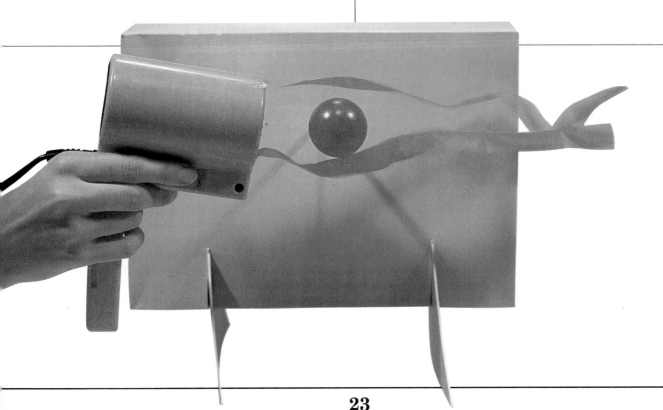

GLIDER FLIGHT

Have you seen a buzzard, a gull, or a kestrel in flight? At times some birds seem to hang in the air without having to flap their wings. Gliders copy these birds, floating on currents of rising air called thermals. Like kites, gliders fly without engine power. However, unlike hot-air balloons, gliders don't just follow the wind. A glider pilot can control the craft by using flaps on the tail and on the wings. The first glider to carry a person was built by an Englishman called Sir George Cayley, in 1853. A state-of-the-art glider, the Space Shuttle gets its lift from the airflow around it. You can make your own simple glider in the project below.

AIRCRAFT DESIGN

1 Study the photographs before you begin. The yellow strips show the flaps and the rudder. The white strips are for double-sided sticky tape.

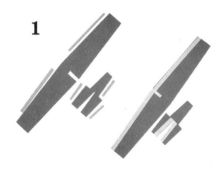

1

2 Make the wings and tail from light, strong, thin oak tag. Cut out the two blue shapes and the five yellow flaps. Your glider can be whatever size you want.

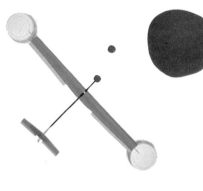

3 Tape on the yellow flaps. Feed a drinking straw through the wings to make an airfoil shape. Use a knitting needle for the body of the glider. Split a 2in piece of straw at one end, and tape it around the tail and onto the knitting needle.

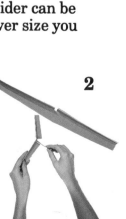

2

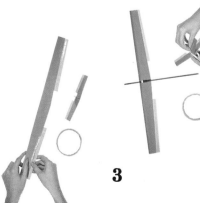

3

BRIGHT IDEAS

-ᗧᗦ- Make your glider "roll." The wings give the glider stability – by moving the wing flaps you can shift its balance.

-ᗧᗦ- You can make your glider climb and dive by moving the flaps on the tail planes.

-ᗧᗦ- A pilot controls the "yaw" with the rudder on the tail. For a yaw to port (a turn to the left), set the rudder as in the picture below. Now try a yaw to starboard (a turn to the right) with your own rudder set as in the picture below.

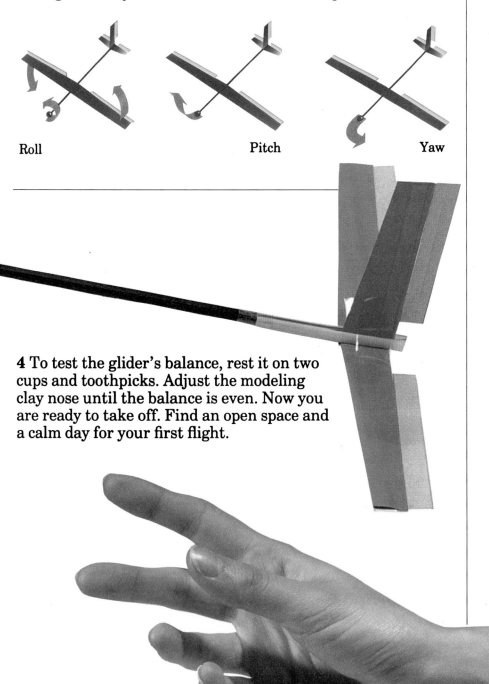

Roll   Pitch   Yaw

4 To test the glider's balance, rest it on two cups and toothpicks. Adjust the modeling clay nose until the balance is even. Now you are ready to take off. Find an open space and a calm day for your first flight.

WHY IT WORKS

Wings and tail flaps help to steer your aircraft. Depending on how these flaps are set (see Bright Ideas), your craft rolls, turns, climbs, or dives as pictured below. This is because the forward motion of the plane is redirected by the force of air hitting the tilted flaps.

Roll

Yaw

Pitch

PROPELLERS AND FANS

Have you ever heard a news report about a hurricane? The power of the wind can be very dangerous, destroying buildings and ripping up trees. If we catch the wind, it can be very helpful, too. Once, windmills used the wind's energy to drive grinding and threshing machinery. Today, smaller, modern windmills make electricity or pump water. The blades of a windmill use the same principle as airplanes, where the special shape of the wing makes them move smoothly in the air. Like sails on a boat, the blades can also turn to catch the wind from every direction.

WORKING WINDMILL

1 To put the power of the wind to work, begin by making holes in a juice carton as shown. Push two straws through the holes, with the bottom straw angling upward.

3

3 Your windmill is going to turn a cam that will push a hammer up. The hammer will strike a table. Make these pieces from stiff cardboard as shown above.

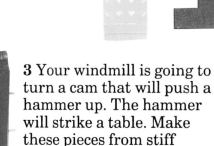

1

2 Make the blades for the propeller by following steps 1 to 3 of the whirligig project on page 28. You will need two pieces of 6in by 5in oak tag. Make the "tail" from the inside of a ballpoint pen.

2

5 To put your simple machine together push the propeller pen through the top straw. The cam wire feeds into this straw from the back.

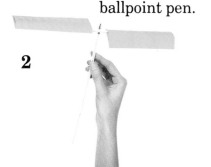

5

4 Tape the L-shaped wire to the yellow cam. Pierce a small hole in the center of the hammer, push the other wire through, and tape it down. Now fold up the "head" of the hammer.

4

6

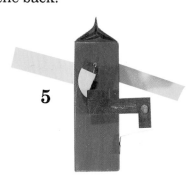

6 The hammer wire feeds into the high end of the bottom straw. Press some modeling clay onto the head. Tape on the table. Now blow on the blades and start your windmill spinning.

BRIGHT IDEAS

Blow on your windmill at different angles as shown here. See which direction makes the blades turn the most quickly and smoothly.

To make a simple paper windmill, you need a square piece of oak tag. Decorate both sides. Cut diagonally from each corner, stopping one-third of the way from the center. Fold down every other point and secure them in the center with a pin. Push the pin through a bead before attaching it to a stick.

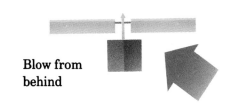

Blow from behind

Blow on side

Blow from front

WHY IT WORKS

The wind passing over the curved edge of your sails has to travel faster than the wind passing over the flat edge. (Remember the airfoil?) The fast moving air has low pressure, which sucks the sails around. Because the airfoils face in opposite directions, the blades are constantly spinning around and around. To correctly catch the airflow from any direction, many windmills have "tails" which turn them to the wind.

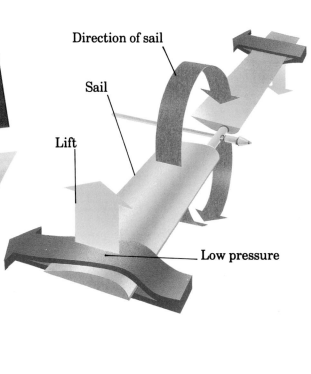

Direction of sail

Sail

Lift

Low pressure

HELICOPTER ACTION

As any object falls through the air, the air pushes against it. Many trees have winged seeds that use this push to make them spin. The wings are shaped like airfoils, so as they spin they stir up low pressure above them. Higher pressure from the blanket of air below slows their fall as they drift away from the "parent tree." Helicopters also get lift from twirling airfoils. Their rotor blades spin so hard that the low pressure creates enough lift to carry them into the air.

WHIRLIGIG

1 Make two small airfoils from two pieces of oak tag, 4in by 3in. Fold each piece with an overlap.

1

2 Push the overlapping edges together and tape them together. One side will curve up like a wing.

2

3 Spread a little glue onto each end of a stiff straw or thin stick. With the curved side of the wings pointing up, glue them onto the straw so that they face in different directions.

3

4 Tape another straw to the one holding the wings. Use a piece of modeling clay to weigh down the end. This keeps the whirligig level.

4

5 To send the whirligig spinning, hold it between the palms of your hands. Brush your hands together, pulling one toward you and pushing the other away. As your hands come apart, the whirligig is released, twirling as it flies.

5

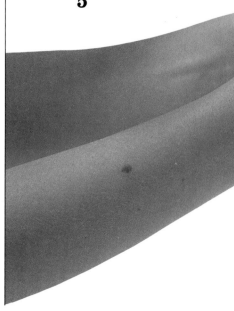

28

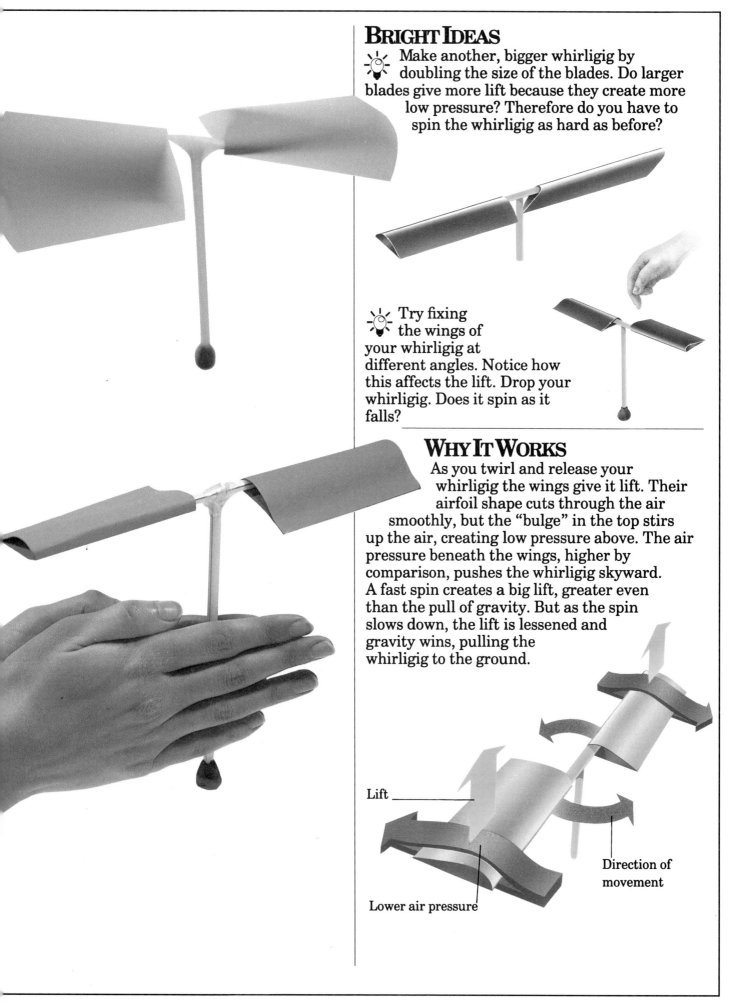

BRIGHT IDEAS

Make another, bigger whirligig by doubling the size of the blades. Do larger blades give more lift because they create more low pressure? Therefore do you have to spin the whirligig as hard as before?

Try fixing the wings of your whirligig at different angles. Notice how this affects the lift. Drop your whirligig. Does it spin as it falls?

WHY IT WORKS

As you twirl and release your whirligig the wings give it lift. Their airfoil shape cuts through the air smoothly, but the "bulge" in the top stirs up the air, creating low pressure above. The air pressure beneath the wings, higher by comparison, pushes the whirligig skyward. A fast spin creates a big lift, greater even than the pull of gravity. But as the spin slows down, the lift is lessened and gravity wins, pulling the whirligig to the ground.

Lift

Direction of movement

Lower air pressure

WATER, PADDLES AND BOATS

INTRODUCTION

Water is familiar to us all, yet it has some strange and beautiful properties. It can stretch and curve. It occurs naturally as solid, liquid, and gas. Sometimes it flows uphill. Most substances contract when cooled, whereas water expands. Thus an ice cube fills more space than it did before freezing. At boiling point, 212 F, water turns to steam, but it requires a large amount of heat for this transformation. Hence, water can store plenty of energy. Harnessed water power is a priceless resource in an age when people must conserve fuel. From the simple wooden waterwheel, engineers developed the water turbine and the steam turbine. These gigantic machines operate generators that provide us with hydroelectric power and sufficient propulsion to drive huge oil tankers. The unharnessed power of water has shaped the face of the earth since time began, carving valleys and coastlines, reshaping and dissolving rocks – even transporting them. The terrible force of tidal waves can unleash devastation on coastal communities. Water covers almost three-quarters of our planet. Made of hydrogen and oxygen, it is the most common compound of basic elements. However simple, plentiful yet precious, water is essential to all living things.

WATER'S CYCLE

Whether falling from a storm cloud or spurting from a kitchen sink, water moves in an endless cycle between Earth and sky. Year after year, the Sun performs a fantastic feat, its energy evaporating 95,000 cubic miles of water from oceans, rivers, lakes, and streams. Rain and snow deliver this water back to Earth. The water cycle is this chain of evaporation and condensation, where water turns to vapor and back to liquid again. Heat accelerates evaporation; cooling leads to condensation. You can illustrate this cycle using hot water and ice.

CLOUDBURST

1 Clean a plastic soda bottle and remove the label. With scissors, carefully cut off the neck and make a wide opening down one side. The opening must be big enough for ice cubes. (Put these in last.)

2 From an empty cereal box cut out the forested mountain slope shown here. Make the front tree section lower than the rear sky section. Paint the scene to look like a real mountainside.

3 Make sure that the bottle fits inside the box as shown. It will be your cloud.

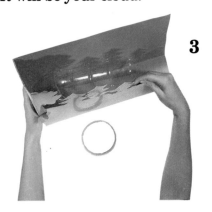

6 Place an aluminum foil dish inside the bottom of the cereal box as shown. Fill the dish with hot water from a kettle. Be careful!

5 Place another sturdy box behind your mountainscape. (It should be the same height.) Tape the wire "handles" to the top of the box.

4 Ask a grown-up to cut a wire coat hanger into two lengths. Curve each piece of wire to fit around the plastic bottle. These metal loops will support the ice-filled bottle.

WHY IT WORKS

The Sun's heat (1) fills molecules, or tiny particles, of surface water with energy, causing them to rise from the mass of water and escape into the air as water vapor (2). Trapped in the cool air, they condense around dust particles as droplets of water. These droplets join as the air cools, forming clouds (3). When the drops become too big and heavy to stay in the air, rain falls (4). The rainwater runs off the land back into the sea in rivers and streams (5).

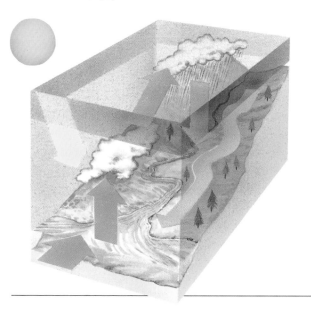

BRIGHT IDEAS

☀ Measure rainfall with a rain gauge. Carefully cut the top off a dishwashing liquid bottle and set it upside down inside the bottom half like a funnel. Mark 1/8- or 1/16-inch divisions from the bottom of the container. Stand it outside in an exposed place. Keep a daily record - remember to empty the gauge every time.

☀ Take two bowls filled to the brim with water. Stand one in a sunny place, the other in the shade. Compare the water levels at the end of each day to measure evaporation.

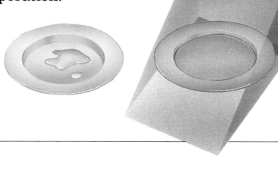

7

7 As the water evaporates from the dish, water vapor will rise and cool. As it cools, it will condense on the plastic ice-filled bottle. Rain will fall!

Freezing And Melting

Not only does water appear as liquid and vapor, but if cooled to freezing point, water turns into a solid. Unlike most substances which shrink when they turn from liquid to solid, water expands. Water is more dense than ice. This is demonstrated by pipes which burst through the expansion of freezing water. Icebergs also give a good clue to the freezing and melting of water. These huge islands of ice adrift in Polar seas have broken off into the sea from vast glaciers or rivers of ice. As ice is 10 percent less dense than water, the top of an iceberg is only one-tenth of the total size of the iceberg. The project below shows how ice floats and how water behaves as it melts.

Melting Iceberg

1 Clean a plastic soda bottle and remove the label. With a sharp pair of scissors carefully cut off the top.

2 Fill a plastic bottle with cold water. Add a few drops of food coloring. Shake the bottle to mix the color well.

3 Pour this colored water into an ice-cube tray. Leave the tray in a freezer to freeze overnight.

4 Pour hot tap water into the large plastic bottle. Add a different coloring and stir.

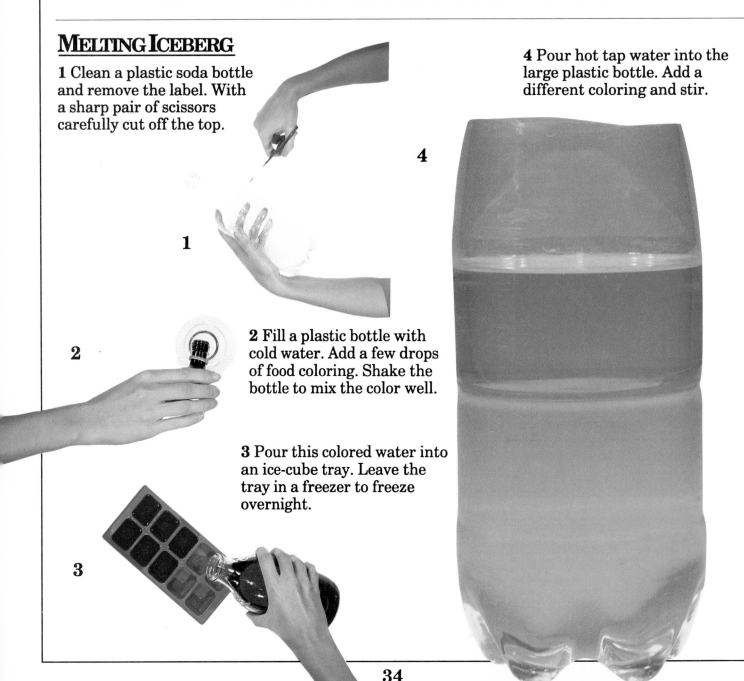

34

WHY IT WORKS

When the ice cube melts, the water sinks as it regains its original density. Also, cold water is denser, or heavier, than hot water and sinks below it. This also causes the cold water melting from the ice cube to sink first to the bottom of the bottle.

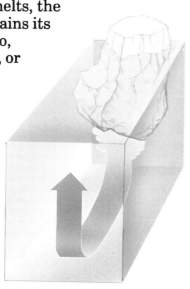

BRIGHT IDEAS

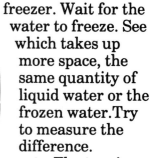

Fill a small plastic bottle to the brim with water and place it uncovered in the freezer. Wait for the water to freeze. See which takes up more space, the same quantity of liquid water or the frozen water. Try to measure the difference.

Float an ice cube in a full glass of water. See if the glass overflows as the ice melts.

5 Drop a colored ice cube in the hot water. Since ice is less dense than water it will float.

6 Watch the water melting off the ice swirl and sink as it regains its liquid density.

5

6

SALTY SOLUTIONS

Most water on the Earth's surface is salty from minerals washed out of rocks by pounding rain and rushing rivers. One such mineral is sodium chloride, or common salt. Salt water is buoyant, which means it can hold things up. It helps boats to float better than they would in fresh water. Israel's Dead Sea, pictured here, is too salty for fish, but is ideal for floating. Salt water is more buoyant because the molecules of salt and water are joined tightly together. You can see how these tightly-knit molecules hold things up better than loosely linked fresh water molecules by trying to float things in both salt and tap water.

FLOATING FISH

1 To make your fish, cut a 1/2-inch thick slice from a washed, medium-sized potato. Cut a triangular tail fin and a semi-circle from colored cellophane.

1

3

2

2 Get an adult to help you make a slit in the potato circle from the center toward the edge. Push the cellophane semicircle through to make balancing fins. Cut another slit along the potato peel for the tail.

3 To make salty water, drop at least 8 large spoonsful of salt in a plastic bottle three-quarters full of cold water. (Note if there is a change in the water level.) Stir the solution with a straw until no more salt will dissolve.

4 Fill a second plastic bottle with the same amount of water as the salt solution. Pour in a few drops of food coloring. Shake it gently to mix the color well.

4

5 Pour the salt solution into a clear bottle from which the top has been cut. Slowly add the colored water by pouring it over the back of a spoon. Place your fish on the water's surface. It will sink no deeper than the surface of salt water.

WHY IT WORKS

Your fish floats in salt water yet sinks in fresh water. This is because the density of the fish is less than the density of the salt water, but more than the fresh water. When you poured salt crystals into the water, the water level did not go up. Instead the salt dissolved and the mixture filled the same space. Therefore, the density of the liquid increased.

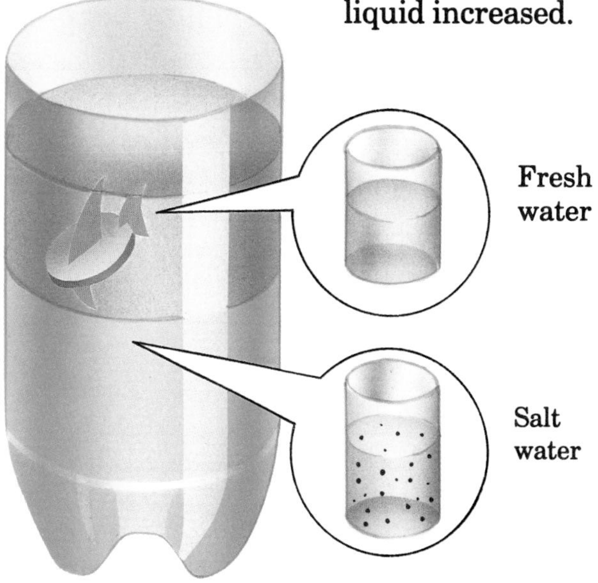

Fresh water

Salt water

BRIGHT IDEAS

You can get the salt back out of the water. Try boiling your solution dry in a saucepan. Be very careful! The salt remains behind. Carefully trap some of the vapor from the boiling solution with the back of a spoon. Watch it condense. The drops of water will be salt-free. Pour all the salt from a salt shaker into a full glass of water. The glass of water will not overflow.

FLOATING LIQUIDS

On a rainy day you will often see oil shimmering on a puddle of water. Like certain objects, liquids, too, can float on other liquids, forming layers as in a salad dressing bottle. Light liquids will float on heavier liquids. Salad oil floats on vinegar because the salad oil is less dense.

Mustard is often added to mix the two solutions as it acts as an emulsifier. Most oils float on water, too. Oil spills can blacken the surface of thousands of miles of water, devastating entire ocean regions and coastlines. One way to disperse a slick and make it mix with water, is to spray it with detergent. You can capture the effect of an oil spill with oil-based paints, water, and paper.

SLICK PICTURES

1

3 Using a clean stick, swirl the colors around. Do this gently on the water's surface. You can make lots of different patterns. When you have made a pattern that you really like, you are ready to capture it as a picture on white paper.

3

1 To make your oil slick pictures you will need some oil-based paints, thinned with turpentine. Choose bright colors to make exciting prints.

4 Lower one sheet of clean, strong paper on top of the paint. Make sure there are no air bubbles. Allow the paint to soak in for a few minutes. Carefully lift the paper off again. Place it on some newspaper to dry.

4

2

2 Fill a deep plastic bowl with cold water. Make sure the bowl is bigger than the sheets of paper you are using for your pictures. (You can add a few drops of vinegar to the water.) Drop small amounts of paint onto the surface of the water.

WHY IT WORKS

Your paints float on the surface because they are less dense than the water below. Liquids of different densities will form into layers in a container, the least dense sitting at the top. To mix the liquids, an emulsifier splits the top layer into tiny droplets that cascade into the layer below. Detergent is an emulsifier that allows oil and water to mix.

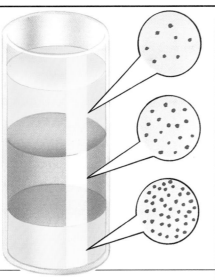

BRIGHT IDEAS

☀ Try pulling the blank paper through the surface paint and wiggling it as you do so. You will have a pattern on both sides of the paper.

☀ Squeeze a few drops of dishwashing liquid onto the surface of the paints. Notice how this changes your marbling pattern.

☀ Pour some oil gently onto the surface of cold water in a screw-top jar. Add dishwashing liquid and shake vigorously. Notice what has happened to the two layers in the jar.

☀ To measure the density of liquids, make an hydrometer with a plastic straw and some modeling clay. Adjust the ball of clay on the bottom of the straw until it will float upright in water. Make a mark on the straw at the surface of the water. Now float it in other liquids and observe the change in levels.

5

5 You can keep making pictures until all the paint is used up. The more pictures you make, the paler the colors will become. Experiment with new designs and colors by dropping more paint onto the surface.

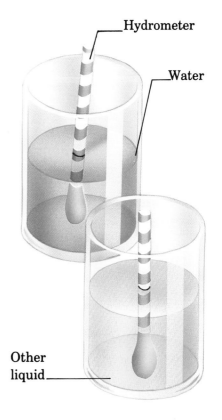

Hydrometer

Water

Other liquid

FLOAT OR SINK?

Enormous aircraft carriers and luxury cruise ships float, yet a single metal screw will sink! Clearly, when it comes to floating, size is not important. Nor necessarily is weight. Whether an object floats or sinks depends on its density and its shape. The Greek mathematician Archimedes noticed that the water level in the bath rose when he got in. He decided that for something to float, the upward push of the water must by the same as the weight of the water displaced, or pushed aside, by the object. Using different objects you can test the rules of floating and sinking.

CRAFTY VESSELS

1 Mold some modeling clay into a solid shape. Try a solid "boat." Drop it into a dish of cold water. Watch it sink to the bottom of the dish. Try other solid shapes, such as a ball.

2 Now use your hands or a rolling pin to roll the clay flat. Curve the edges up to make a boat. Be sure that there are no holes or it will leak!

1

2

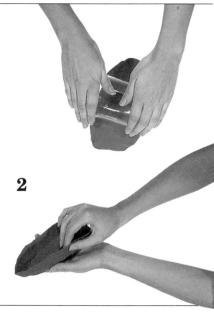

3 Half fill a shallow dish with cold water. Gently place your boat onto the surface of the water. It will float easily unless there is a leak. Check how low in the water your boat sits. Mark a water level line on the side of the boat. If you want the boat to carry a load safely, it must sit high in the water.

BRIGHT IDEAS

💡 Can you make your boat even more sea-worthy? Mold different shapes. A high-sided shape floats better than a shallow one. Make a long-shaped boat and a round-shaped one. See how many passengers your boat will carry. Try different loads. Mark a safe water level on your craft. This is called a plimsoll line after Samuel Plimsoll.

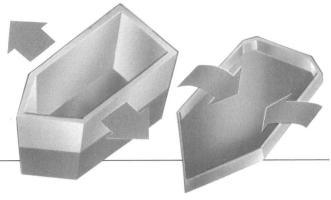

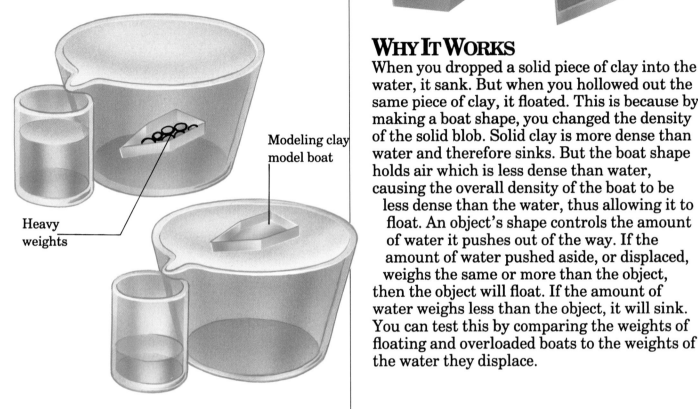

Heavy weights

Modeling clay model boat

WHY IT WORKS

When you dropped a solid piece of clay into the water, it sank. But when you hollowed out the same piece of clay, it floated. This is because by making a boat shape, you changed the density of the solid blob. Solid clay is more dense than water and therefore sinks. But the boat shape holds air which is less dense than water, causing the overall density of the boat to be less dense than the water, thus allowing it to float. An object's shape controls the amount of water it pushes out of the way. If the amount of water pushed aside, or displaced, weighs the same or more than the object, then the object will float. If the amount of water weighs less than the object, it will sink. You can test this by comparing the weights of floating and overloaded boats to the weights of the water they displace.

4

4 Now make a modeling clay passenger. Sit your passenger in the middle of the boat so that it doesn't tip over. (The one shown here is gripping the sides to stay balanced.) Put the boat back in the water and watch it float with the new load. The water level will change. See if it sits lower in the water than the empty boat.

CURVING WATER

A glass of water can be more than full without overflowing. The water seems to puff above the rim of the glass as if held by an invisible skin. Dew drops on a leaf appear to have this skin and so does water at the surface of a still pond. The water strider can glide at great speed over this taut film on the top of water. If you dip the bristles of a paintbrush in water they will spread out. When you lift it out again, they pull together. Each of these effects arise from surface tension, the force between molecules at the surface of all water. You can test its strength yourself.

WATER WALKERS

1 To make your water insects you will need some lightweight aluminum foil and some paper clips. Use sharp scissors to cut the foil into small pieces, one for each paper clip. Make a number of insects so that you can experiment. You can vary the size of your insects.

2 Place a paper clip in the middle of one half of each piece of foil. Fold over the other half of the foil so that the paper clip is enclosed. With your fingers, shape six legs on each insect. Look at the insects in the picture opposite.

3 Half fill a shallow dish with cold water. Very gently lower each insect onto the water's surface.

4. You can position all of your insects on the water at once. To do this you need a paper tissue. Place your insects on the tissue. Holding it firmly at each end, lower the tissue until it rests on the surface of the water.

WHY IT WORKS

Water molecules attract each other. Surface molecules have no water molecules attracting them from above so they pull together extra hard at the sides. The result is a force called surface tension - strong enough to support certain insects. Dishwashing liquid reduces this surface tension by breaking down the forces of attraction between the water molecules.

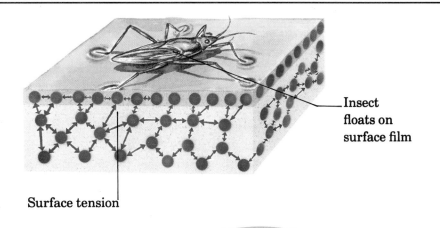

Insect floats on surface film

Surface tension

6 When the water is still, carefully drop some dishwashing liquid onto the surface, just behind each insect. Watch them dart about! To repeat, you need fresh water.

5 The tissue will soak up water and gradually sink to the bottom. But the insects will rest on the surface. Before making your insects dart over the water make sure the liquid is absolutely still.

6

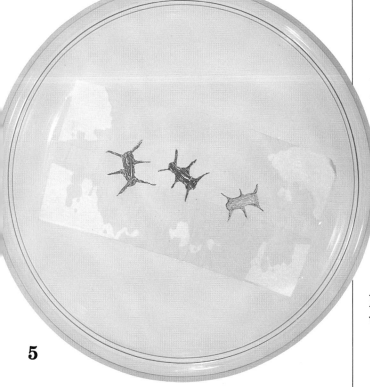

5

BRIGHT IDEAS

☀ Float your insects together in the center of the bowl and carefully drop some dishwashing liquid on the water between them. Watch the skaters dart away.

☀ Sprinkle talcum powder onto a shallow dish full of water. Touch the water in one spot with dishwashing liquid and see what happens.

Dishwashing liquid

43

DIVING DEEP

Submarines were once the creation of science fiction. Today, underwater vessels map the ocean floor, repair oil rigs, and fire torpedoes. There is even a home for aquanauts beneath the sea! To dive and resurface, submarines have borrowed their design from nature. Some jellyfish, usually seen at the surface, can sink into the deep by deflating the air sac that aids their propulsion. In the same way, submarine tanks take in water to go down and replace it with air to rise up again. This kind of diving and resurfacing is possible because water is heavier than air, and water-filled objects will always sink. Try it yourself with a jellyfish that takes in water to dive and expels it to resurface.

PLUNGING JELLYFISH

1 To make the jellyfish, you will need a bendable plastic straw, a paper clip and some modeling clay. Bend the ribbed part of the straw and cut the long side to the same length as the short side.

1

2 Bend a paper clip as shown here. Insert the bent paper clip into each end of the straw. Push the paper clip firmly inside, making sure that it will not slide out.

2

3 Roll out three thin strips of clay. Loop and pinch each one around the paper clip.

3

4 Test your jellyfish in a clear cup of water to make sure that it will float the right side up. If it doesn't, try adding more clay. This will give it weight and balance. Place it to sit as shown here.

4

5 Float your jellyfish in a large bottle full of water. Screw on the top.

5

WHY IT WORKS

When you squeeze the bottle, water is pushed into the plastic straw, compressing the air. Because water weighs more than air, the jellyfish gets heavier, causing it to sink.

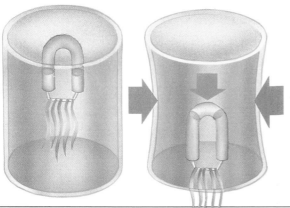

BRIGHT IDEAS

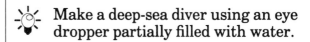 Instead of using a screw-top bottle, try using a deep plastic container to house your jellyfish. Stretch plastic wrap over the top and secure with a rubber band. Apply some pressure to the cling film. Which works best?

Make a deep-sea diver using an eye dropper partially filled with water.

Try floating a plastic bottle filled with varying amounts of water. Try filling it half full or three-quarters full. See how easy it is to submerge with these different amounts of water.

6 Squeeze the sides of the plastic bottle hard. The jellyfish will sink to the bottom as water enters the straw, compressing the air inside it. This makes the jellyfish heavier.

7 Releasing the pressure on the sides of the bottle allows the jellyfish to rise to the surface again. The compressed air inside the straw expands again, forcing the water back out. The jellyfish becomes lighter and therefore more buoyant.

HYDRAULIC MUSCLE

Water can be made to lift heavy things. Because water and other liquids cannot be squeezed, if they are thrust through pipes, they will carry a powerful force. In the 17th century, Blaise Pascal was the first person to discover the principles of hydraulics. Hydraulic lifts are machines that use the natural pushing power of liquids to raise loads. Most modern hydraulic lifts use oil instead of water. Excavating machines operate hydraulic rams. Cars have hydraulic brakes. In the 1930's, the fire services reached greater heights by introducing hydraulically operated turntable ladders. Today, disabled skiers make use of a hydraulic skibob with hydraulic suspension. You can make your own hydraulic lift simply by linking two water-filled containers.

LIQUID LIFT

1 Using sharp scissors, carefully cut the tops off two bottles. Make them the same height.

2 Pierce a hole in the side of each bottle about 2 inches from the bottom. Link the two bottles by inserting the plastic straw into the holes. Use the clay as a seal; there should be no leaks when the bottles are filled with water.

3 You need a balloon, a plastic cup, and some clay. Place the clay inside the cup.

4 Fill the bottles with cold water to the level shown in the picture, about three-quarters full. You can add food coloring to see the water levels more clearly. Place the weighted cup on the surface of the water in one of the containers. Experiment with different weights of clay. It must float. This will be your load.

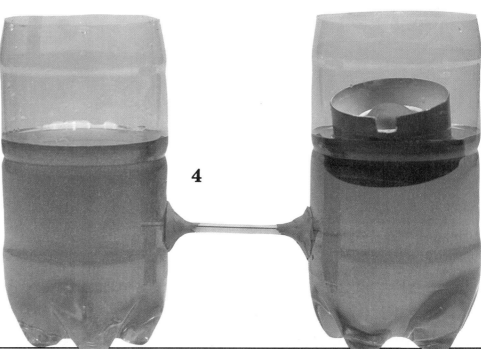

WHY IT WORKS

Unlike air, liquids cannot be compressed, or squeezed; any pressure that is applied to them passes through the liquid in every direction without loss of strength. When you push down on one side of your water lift, the water has no place to go but up the other side. Pressure from the rising water raises the load.

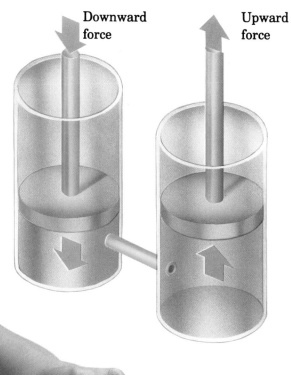

Downward force

Upward force

BRIGHT IDEAS

🔅 Increase the load to be lifted. Try several different weights. Test to see if they can be raised as high as each other. Push the balloon down to the same level every time!

🔅 Now make a different type of water lift. Replace one bottle with a taller, narrower bottle. See if a load in this new bottle can be raised higher. Notice what happens if you put the load in the other side.

🔅 Try making an oil lift. Pour the water out of both containers and replace it with cooking oil. Does this lift work as well or better than the water lift? Oil is messy stuff, so be sure to clean up thoroughly!

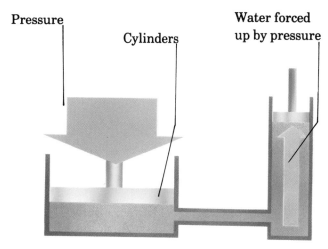

Pressure

Cylinders

Water forced up by pressure

5

5 Position the inflated balloon on the surface of the water and gently push it down. As you push the water down on one side it rises up the other side, lifting the load. The balloon acts as a piston. To raise the load even higher, you need to put more pressure on the balloon. Note the water levels in both bottles. If the water under the balloon goes down by a certain amount, observe how far it goes up on the other side.

WATER ENGINEERING

For thousands of years people have used water's pushing power to drive machines. Since Roman times wooden waterwheels have powered millstones to grind corn. Later, waterwheels became the main power source for industry. One of the largest machines in the world, the modern water turbine, was developed from the waterwheel. Water turbines are harnessed to generators to produce hydroelectric power. With all waterwheels, the flow of water is directed around wheel blades to start the wheel spinning. The constant movement from the revolving wheel can then be put to work. You can make a waterwheel go to work for you. This one raises a bucketful of water.

WATER ENGINEERING

2

1 Cut the bottom from a dishwashing liquid bottle to make a waterwheel. Cut out 4 evenly-spaced flaps around the sides of the bottle and fold them out as shown.

1

4

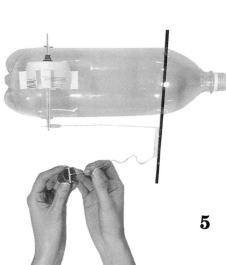

2 Make a hole in the base of the waterwheel and insert a straw. Secure it in place with clay. Cut a section from a soda bottle large enough for the waterwheel to sit inside. Pierce two holes on either side of the bottle for the straw to pass through.

3

3 Fit the waterwheel into the cutout section of the bottle, easing the straw through the holes. Poke toothpicks through the straw to secure it in place.

4 Make two holes through the top of the bottle and insert a pencil or chopstick. Tape a short piece of straw to the end of the pencil.

5 Make a bucket from a bottle cap. Glue a matchstick across the top. Tie it to thread.

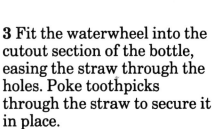

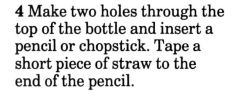

5

6 Feed the thread through the short straw on the pencil and tie it to the waterwheel straw. Cut the base off a dishwashing liquid container. Join it upside down to the soda bottle with clay, making sure the top is off. Stand the whole thing inside a large bowl. Now fill the detergent bottle with water. Watch the waterwheel work as the falling water hits the blades. It will raise the "bucket" for you.

6

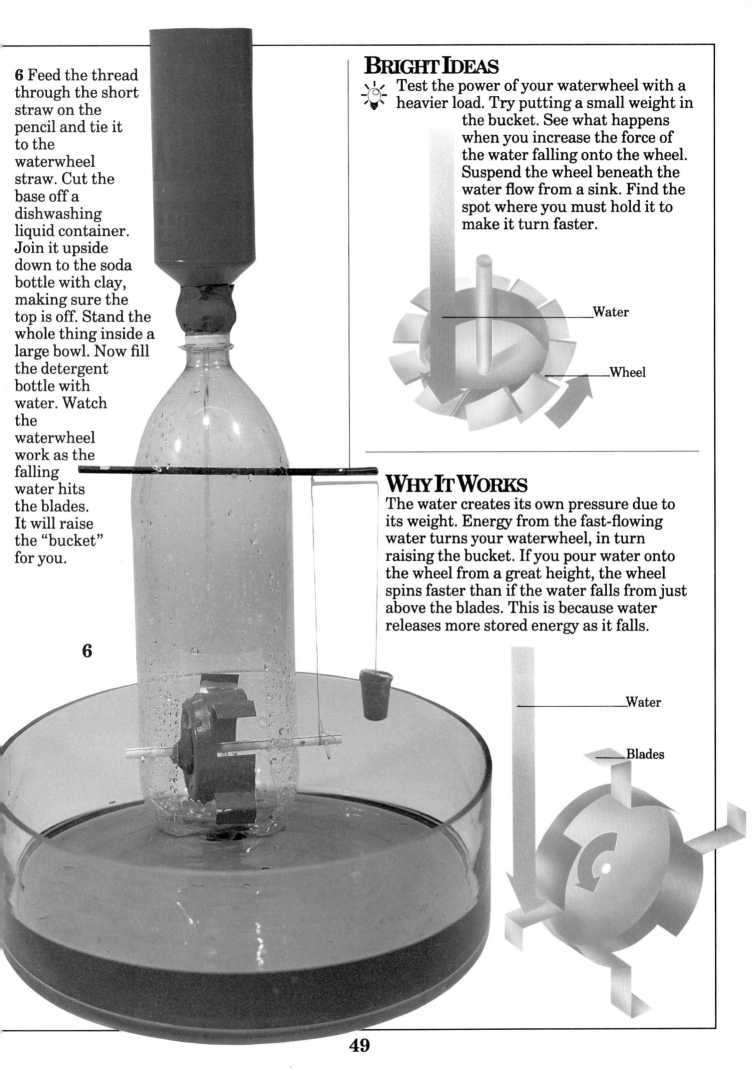

BRIGHT IDEAS

Test the power of your waterwheel with a heavier load. Try putting a small weight in the bucket. See what happens when you increase the force of the water falling onto the wheel. Suspend the wheel beneath the water flow from a sink. Find the spot where you must hold it to make it turn faster.

Water

Wheel

WHY IT WORKS

The water creates its own pressure due to its weight. Energy from the fast-flowing water turns your waterwheel, in turn raising the bucket. If you pour water onto the wheel from a great height, the wheel spins faster than if the water falls from just above the blades. This is because water releases more stored energy as it falls.

Water

Blades

PADDLE POWER

The first paddles used for moving vessels in water were probably simple oars. By the early nineteenth century the first steam-powered ships were fitted with paddles. As the paddle circled around and around, it pushed back the water with its blades. This action propelled the vessel forward. It was Isaac Newton who first stated that for every action, such as the paddle pushing against the water, there is an equal and opposite reaction – the vessel being propelled forward. The British engineer Isambard Kingdom Brunel built the first iron ship to be driven by a screw propeller which, like the paddle, pushes the water backward and the ship forward. Today, paddle steamers, like the one pictured here, still carry tourists on the Mississippi River. You can make a model boat that is powered the same way.

SPEEDY BOATS

1 Take a small plastic bottle with a top and cut a hole in one side large enough for a cardboard tube. This cardboard tube will be the funnel of your paddle steamer.

2 Tape two sticks or pencils on either side of the bottle. They should stick out about 2 inches past the bottom of the bottle.

3 Cut two rectangles from a fruit juice carton. Make sure they are smaller than the base of the bottle.

4 Make a slit halfway down the middle of each. Slide them together to form a paddle.

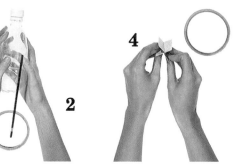

WHY IT WORKS

The paddleboat is driven by the potential, or hidden, energy stored in the rubber band. As the rubber band unwinds, the paddle turns, pushing the water backward and the boat forward. The potential energy has been changed into kinetic, or moving, energy.

BRIGHT IDEAS

Find out how far the boat travels in relation to the number of turns that you give the paddle. You can make a graph to show the results. See if winding up the paddle in or out of the water makes any difference.

Twist the paddle clockwise and note what happens when the boat moves. Now twist it counterclockwise. Attach a different rubber band to your boat. Notice if a tighter rubber band changes the boat's motion.

Make a propeller-driven boat. See if it goes farther or faster than a paddle-driven boat. Race your two different types of boat together in the bathtub.

6 Place the paddle wheel in between the sticks. Loop the ends of the rubber band around each stick. Make sure that the paddle wheel is not touching the bottle.

7 Weight the boat down with clay. Fit a cardboard tube in the hole. Wind up the paddle around the rubber band and place the boat in the water. Let go and watch it shoot forward.

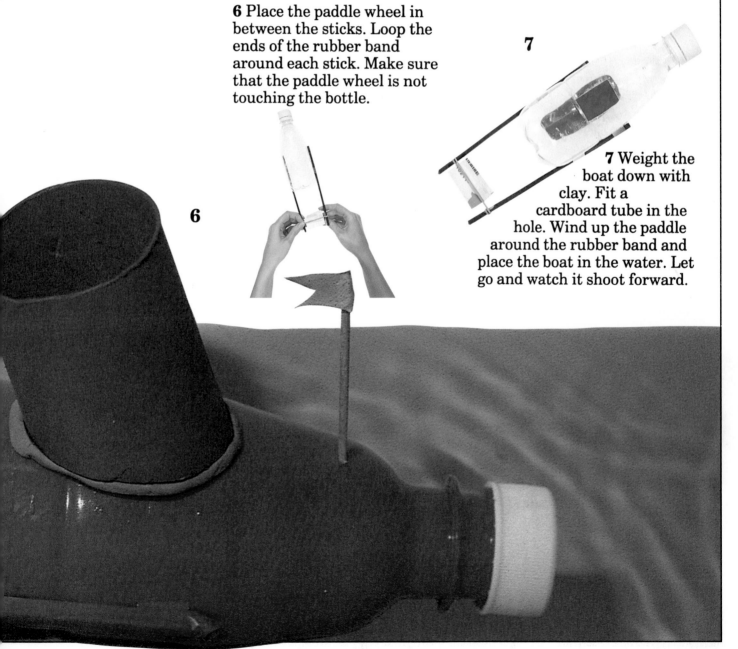

STEERING AND BALANCE

The Vikings used a single, hand-operated steering oar at the stern, or back, of their ships. Always on the right-hand side, it led to the term steerboard, or starboard. Stern rudders were first used over 1,000 years ago on flat-bottomed Chinese junks. Modern propeller-driven submarines are steered by tail rudders. To maneuver up and down, they use hydroplane fins which look like airplane wings. Dolphins are propelled by their tail fins – the other fins are for balance and steering.

RUDDER DESIGN

1 For your rudder, slide a pipe cleaner inside a straw, leaving a piece sticking out at the top for the handle and a piece at the bottom.

2 Cut out the shape for the rudder from a fruit juice container. Attach it to the straight end of the pipe cleaner. Make sure it points in the opposite direction to the handle.

3 Attach the finished rudder to the back of your paddleboat with modeling clay. Wind the paddle counterclockwise to propel the boat through the water. Once it is moving, use the handle of the rudder to change the direction in which it travels. Keep a record of what happens. When you push the handle to the right, observe which way the rudder turns. At the same time, notice which way this makes the boat turn.

3

BRIGHT IDEAS

If you want to turn the boat to starboard, which way must you turn the rudder? See if you can make your boat do a complete turn by operating the rudder.

Make a "submarine" and fit four adjustable curved fins to the sides. To maneuver, or turn, your vessel, experiment with the fins. With the back fins and the front fins curving in the same direction, gently drop the submarine in water. Now test what happens when the fins are fixed in different directions. For example, try the front fins curving up and the back fins curving down.

WHY IT WORKS

If the rudder is pointing in the same direction as the flow of water, the ship moves straight ahead (3). If the flow strikes the rudder at an angle (1,2), the ship turns. As the force of the flow tries to push the angled rudder back to parallel, it is met with resistance - an opposing force that turns the boat.

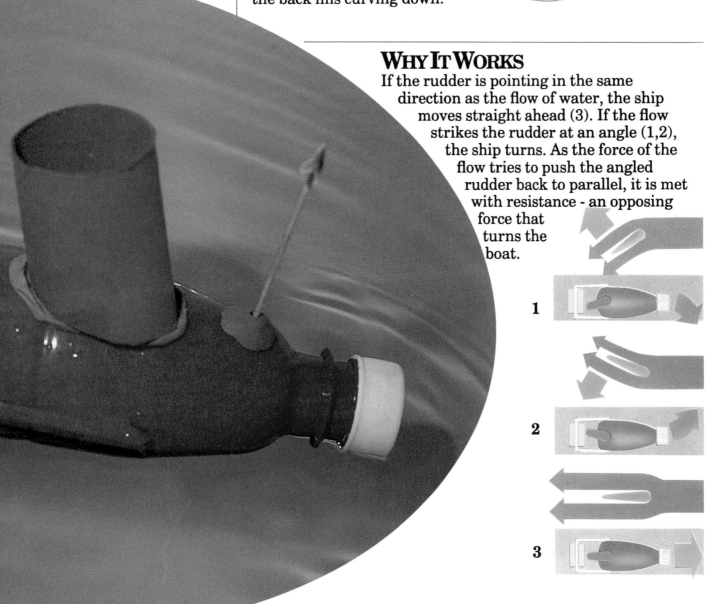

1

2

3

ELECTRICITY

INTRODUCTION

Electricity, natural and generated, touches every aspect of our lives. Electricity makes our bodies work as electric currents carry messages along nerves inside us. In some animals, like the electric ray, a strong electric current can be generated to ward off enemies. Electricity can be converted into heat and light, it can magnetize, and it can be transformed into mechanical energy. So many things we do today are made easier by electricity. It enables us to cook, wash, and clean without effort, it powers the machines that entertain us and the trains we travel in. It even allows us to communicate across the world instantaneously. Electrical equipment fills almost every home. Soon we will see a computer that can store X-rays, a compact disc that can record videos, even a videophone. Yet there are still parts of the world where electricity is nonexistent or unreliable. Areas that do not receive main-line electricity may rely on wind, water, or solar power. These sources of energy may be used more extensively in the future. For although electricity is clean to use, it is usually generated by fuels that are not.

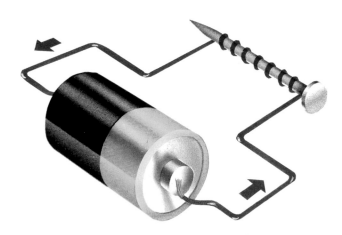

NATURAL ELECTRICITY

Thousands of years ago, the Greeks noticed that a type of stone called amber attracted light-weight objects, like feathers, after it was rubbed. The Greek word for amber is "elektron." Some materials, such as plastic, do not let electricity pass through, but if they rub against another material, a charge of static electricity can be produced. Static means staying in the same place. We experience static daily – you may hear a crackling sound when you take off your sweater. Sometimes a spark is produced. Rubbing or friction causes static. You can generate your own static and watch the frogs jump.

ACTIVE AMPHIBIANS!

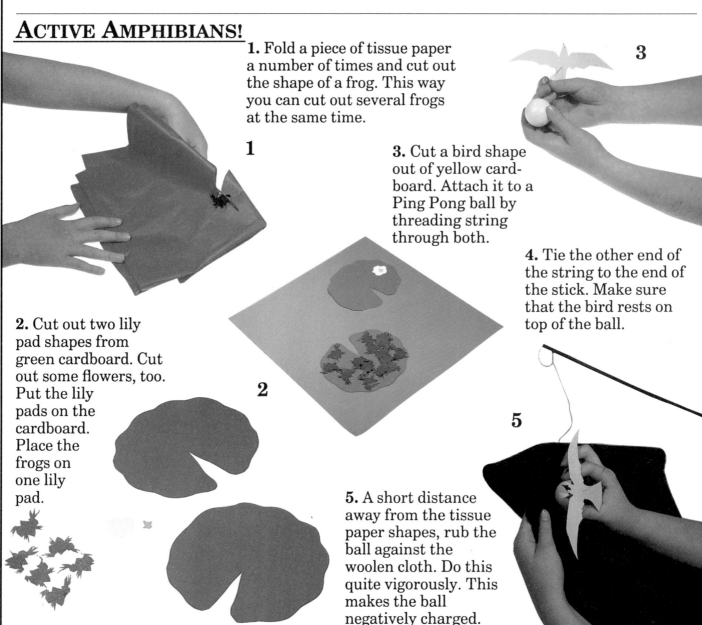

1. Fold a piece of tissue paper a number of times and cut out the shape of a frog. This way you can cut out several frogs at the same time.

2. Cut out two lily pad shapes from green cardboard. Cut out some flowers, too. Put the lily pads on the cardboard. Place the frogs on one lily pad.

3. Cut a bird shape out of yellow card-board. Attach it to a Ping Pong ball by threading string through both.

4. Tie the other end of the string to the end of the stick. Make sure that the bird rests on top of the ball.

5. A short distance away from the tissue paper shapes, rub the ball against the woolen cloth. Do this quite vigorously. This makes the ball negatively charged.

WHY IT WORKS

The paper clips act as switches. Both must be in contact with the drawing pins to allow electrons to flow around the whole circuit, lighting up the bulbs. The sender must raise and lower one paper clip to turn the bulb on and off – the receiver must keep the other down to complete the circuit.

A mechanical switch in the home is slow to work and produces a spark. It joins and separates electrical contacts in the circuit. The spark or arcing produced creates high temperatures. A relay is an electrically controlled switch; it can be operated by various means, but the most common is an electromagnet called a solenoid (see page 74). The solenoid uses an electromagnet to move a metal rod through a short distance. This opens or closes the relay circuit.

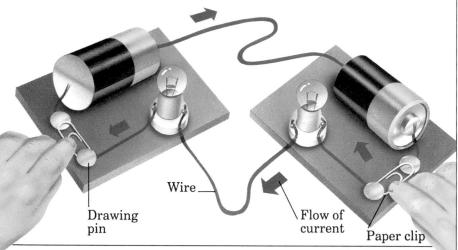

Drawing pin

Wire

Flow of current

Paper clip

4. Rest two batteries end to end on each board and connect them into the circuit using modeling clay. Check to see that the bulbs work by holding down both clips.

5. The bulbs are connected in series. When one bulb lights, both light. A gap in the circuit and the bulbs will not glow.

BRIGHT IDEAS

S.O.S. is 3 short, 3 long, 3 short flashes – now try sending a whole message. Find a copy of the Morse Code. Can you "translate" a reply? Can you build a two-way circuit that will work from another room? If you use bulbs, the wiring must be long enough to link the two. See what happens to the light from the bulb if you use longer wire. How can you tell when each word and sentence ends? Try working out a special code, then you can send secret messages.

Make a burglar alarm system with a pressure switch made out of folded aluminum foil. Hide the switch underneath a rug and connect it into an electrical circuit with a buzzer or bulb. Which kind of alarm do you think is most effective – a bulb or buzzer?

How many switches are there in your home? Where are they? What does each switch operate? Carry out a survey.

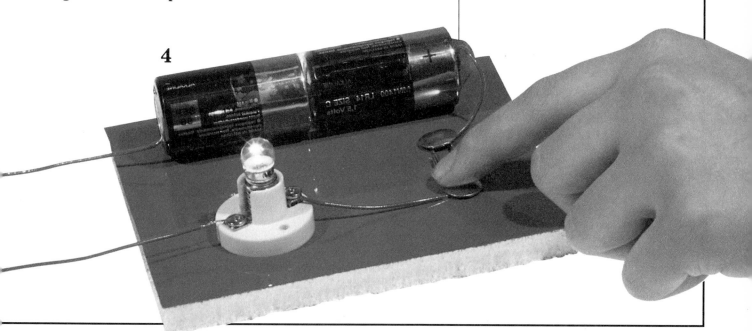

4

SWITCHES AND ENERGY

Most modern gadgets, such as hair dryers and toasters, switch off automatically. This is not only important to conserve energy, but is a safety precaution too. Heating appliances, such as stoves and irons, have thermostats so that a selected temperature can be maintained – an internal switch turns the heater on or off as required. Because most of our electricity is generated from sources of energy like coal which will run out, we must be aware of the need to save energy whenever possible. The two-way switch is important today, both as a safety device and as a means of conserving energy. If a light can be switched on or off from the top or the bottom of a staircase, not only is it safer at night, but light energy can be saved. Make your own two-way switch and discover how it works.

SWITCH OFF!

1. Position drawing pins at either end of a board so that two plastic lids can just turn, like knobs, within them.

2. Align four pins as shown and connect them in pairs with two lengths of wire. Make a hole in the top of one plastic knob and insert the two wires connected to a bulb holder.

3. Connect one wire to a paper clip inserted through the lid, as shown, taking the other to the batteries.

4. Form a switch at the other lid in the same way, connecting the wire to the batteries. Modeling clay will hold the wires in place.

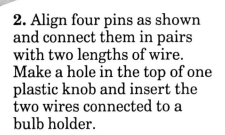

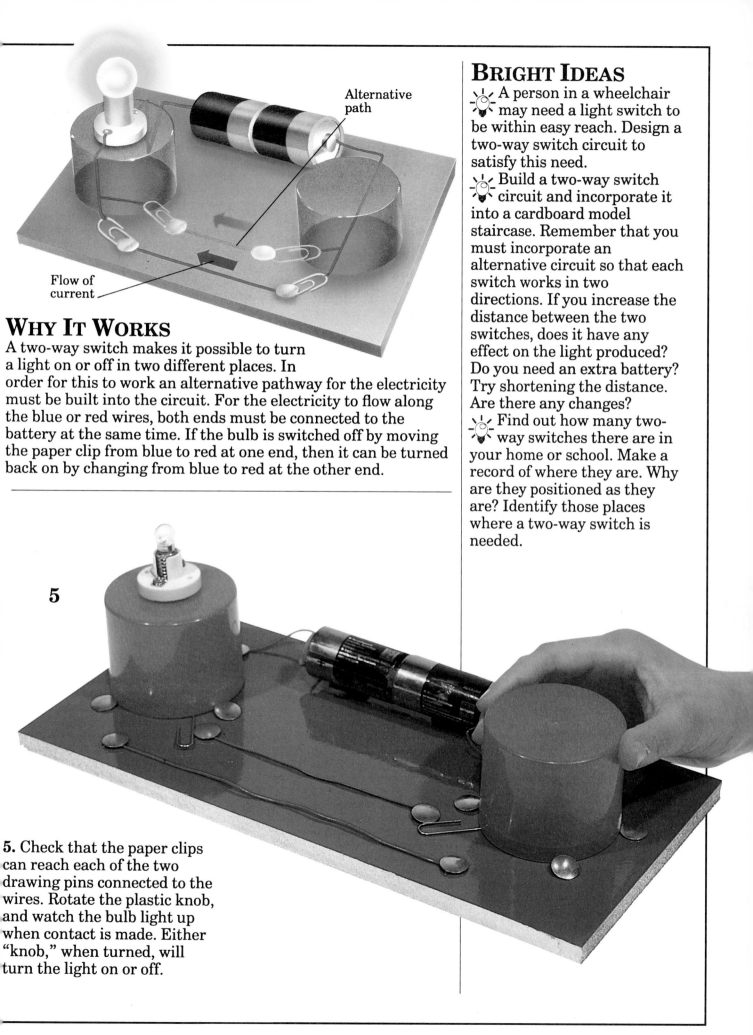

Alternative
path

Flow of
current

WHY IT WORKS

A two-way switch makes it possible to turn
a light on or off in two different places. In
order for this to work an alternative pathway for the electricity
must be built into the circuit. For the electricity to flow along
the blue or red wires, both ends must be connected to the
battery at the same time. If the bulb is switched off by moving
the paper clip from blue to red at one end, then it can be turned
back on by changing from blue to red at the other end.

BRIGHT IDEAS

A person in a wheelchair
may need a light switch to
be within easy reach. Design a
two-way switch circuit to
satisfy this need.

Build a two-way switch
circuit and incorporate it
into a cardboard model
staircase. Remember that you
must incorporate an
alternative circuit so that each
switch works in two
directions. If you increase the
distance between the two
switches, does it have any
effect on the light produced?
Do you need an extra battery?
Try shortening the distance.
Are there any changes?

Find out how many two-
way switches there are in
your home or school. Make a
record of where they are. Why
are they positioned as they
are? Identify those places
where a two-way switch is
needed.

5

5. Check that the paper clips
can reach each of the two
drawing pins connected to the
wires. Rotate the plastic knob,
and watch the bulb light up
when contact is made. Either
"knob," when turned, will
turn the light on or off.

BULBS

The warning flashes of lighthouses are vital to the safety of ships around the coastline. It was not until the mid-nineteenth century that lighthouses were equipped with electric light bulbs. Two men were responsible for the invention of the incandescent (white-hot) electric light bulb; Thomas Edison, an American, and Joseph Swan, an Englishman. Edison's light bulbs contained a carbon filament within a vacuum. He first produced this on October 21, 1879. By 1913, the tungsten filament (a type of metal) that is still used today had been introduced. Neon lights, like those pictured here, contain a gas. When electricity is passed through the gas, the tube glows. Electronic bulbs have also been developed. These produce only light – not heat – and so save energy.

DANGER AT SEA!

1

3. Use a long cardboard tube for your lighthouse. Cut a piece of polystyrene to fit the end and place the candle through the middle, as shown.

4. Insert the whole thing into the top of your lighthouse, allowing the wires to hang out of the end.

4

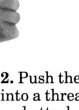

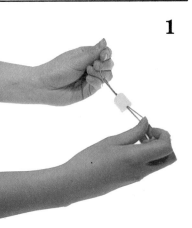

3

1. Take a piece of candle and make a hole down the center. Use a paper clip to thread a rubber band through.

2

5. Fix the polystyrene, candle, and rubber band in place with two toothpicks. Push them right through the cardboard tube, from one side to the other.

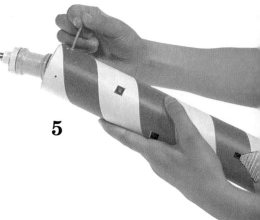

6. Line a plastic cup with aluminum foil. Cut out a window to see the bulb. A piece of cardboard with a hole to fit over the bulb will hold it in place.

2. Push the candle into a thread spool and attach the band to the top with tape. Also attach a bulb in a holder to the top, passing the wires down through the candle.

5

WHY IT WORKS

As the bulb puts the electrons to work by making it travel through a very long, thin wire called the filament, electric energy is transferred into light energy. Tungsten is a highly resistant metal that can become white hot without melting. Air is removed from the bulb and replaced by the harmless gas, argon. Electrons flow into the bulb when the circuit is complete and cause the wire to glow. Metal at the base of the bulb makes contact with the circuit. Bulbs can become very hot when switched on.

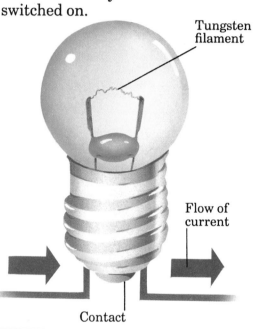

Tungsten filament

Flow of current

Contact

BRIGHT IDEAS

☀ Can you make a different kind of flashing light without switching the current off and on? Adapt the project to make the light revolve and flash in a different way. Try using colored cellophane in the window to make a colored light. Another way to make a flashing light is to use a circle of cardboard, out of which slits like the spokes of a wheel have been cut. Place it in front of the bulb – then revolve the cardboard when the bulb is glowing.

☀ Design and build a traffic light circuit so that the bulbs can be switched on and off in particular sequence. The sequence of change is different in various countries.

☀ Do you know what causes a fluorescent strip light to flicker? The answer has to do with the fact that main-line electricity uses an alternating current (a current that varies all the time).

☀ Design a poster encouraging people to turn lights off and save energy.

7

7. Connect the wires to a battery and hide it under a papier mâché "rock." Add cotton ball waves. Now twist the thread spool around several times, let go and watch the warning light turn.

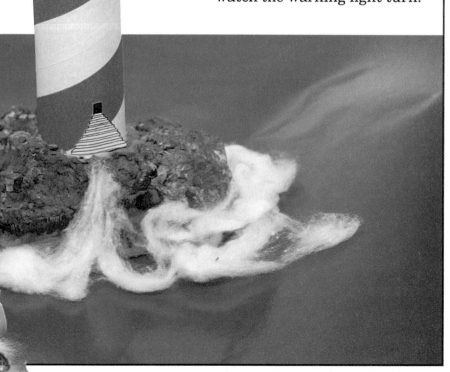

INSULATORS AND CONDUCTORS

Our bodies can conduct electricity, especially when they are wet. Never touch plugs, sockets, or light switches with wet hands. A conductor will allow electricity to pass through it. We use conductors to take electricity to where it is needed. We use insulators to prevent it from reaching places where it could be dangerous. Electricians, like the one pictured here, wear rubber boots to protect themselves from electric shocks. Metal wires conducting electricity are insulated with rubber or plastic to make them safe. Conduct your way through a maze, using insulators and conductors as your guides.

AMAZING!

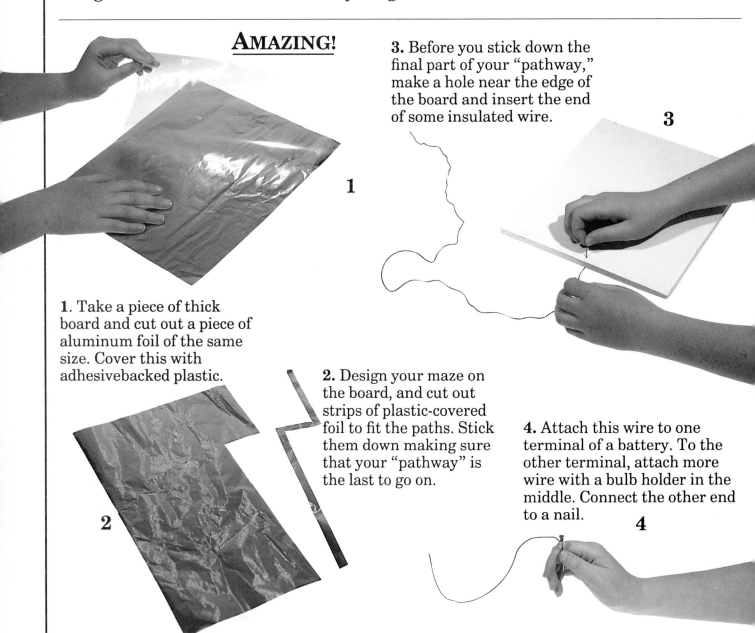

1. Take a piece of thick board and cut out a piece of aluminum foil of the same size. Cover this with adhesivebacked plastic.

2. Design your maze on the board, and cut out strips of plastic-covered foil to fit the paths. Stick them down making sure that your "pathway" is the last to go on.

3. Before you stick down the final part of your "pathway," make a hole near the edge of the board and insert the end of some insulated wire.

4. Attach this wire to one terminal of a battery. To the other terminal, attach more wire with a bulb holder in the middle. Connect the other end to a nail.

WHY IT WORKS

The aluminum foil conducts electricity and allows the circuit to be completed. The bulb glows. But when the nail touches the plastic covering in the maze, the bulb goes out. Plastic is an insulator. A substance that conducts electricity must contain charged particles that are free to move around. These free electrons pass on the current. The electrons in the plastic cannot move.

BRIGHT IDEAS

Build a simple circuit leaving a gap between two wires. Collect a variety of materials and test each in the gap. Ensure that contact is made with the material by each of the bared wires. Which one makes the bulb light up? Record your results. Make separate lists. Which materials are insulators, which are conductors? Do some materials conduct electricity better than others? How can you tell?

Look at objects around you, such as tools and electrical equipment. Notice which have insulating material on them. Why is it necessary to insulate objects like this?

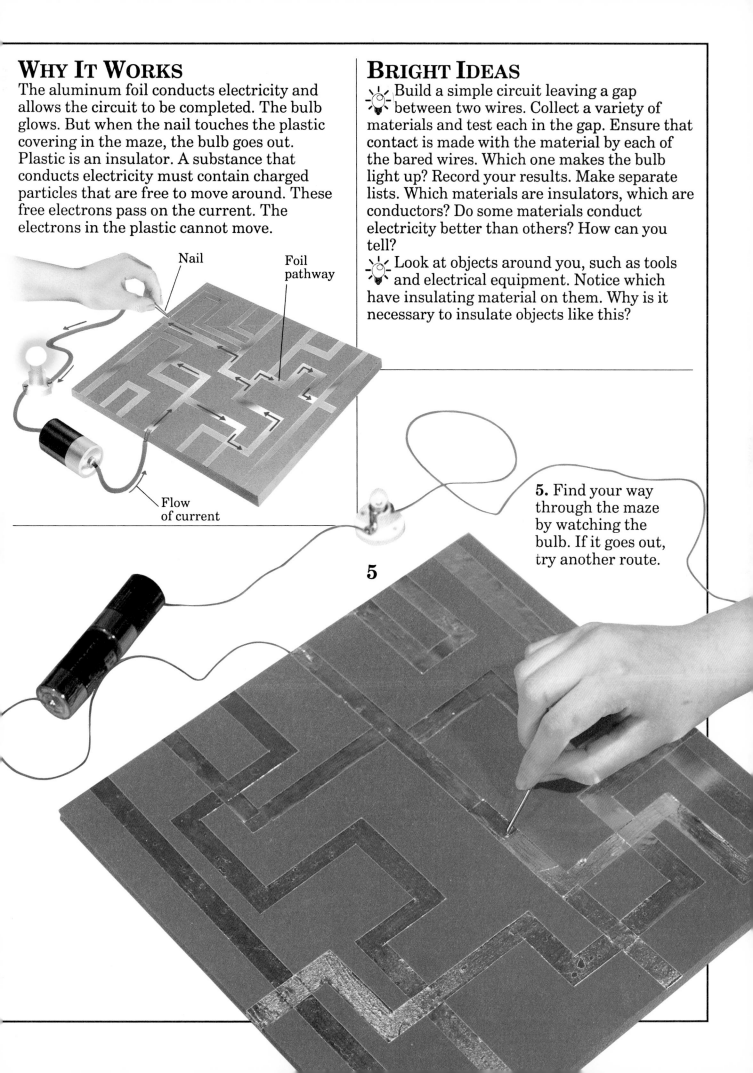

Nail

Foil pathway

Flow of current

5. Find your way through the maze by watching the bulb. If it goes out, try another route.

5

ELECTRICAL RESISTANCE

James Watt, inventor of the steam engine, gave his name to the measurement of electrical power, the watt. Electrical resistance is what makes the filament (long, thin piece of wire) in a bulb glow and the element in an electric heater become hot.

Resistance is measured in ohms, after the German scientist, Georg Simon Ohm. Resistors are used in circuits, like the ones pictured here. They are coils of wire, or poor conductors, built into the circuit to reduce the current. A variable resistor, or rheostat, is used to control the speed of a toy car and the volume of a radio or television. By building your own resistor, you can make a night-light with a dimmer switch.

DIM THE LIGHT

1. Set up a circuit using a bulb in a holder, insulated wire, a board, and safety pins. Ask an adult to cut the lead out of a pencil, and cut out two pieces of thick cardboard to rest it on.

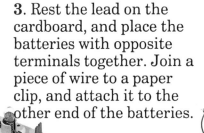

4. To reflect the light, make a shade of cardboard and aluminum foil. Cut a slit in the flat disk and glue it into a cone shape.

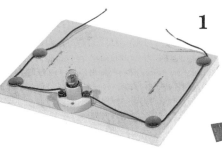

1

5. Cut a hole in the center of the cone and place it over the bulb. Slip the paper clip over the pencil lead and watch the bulb light up.

2. Attach one end of the wire to the batteries and the other end to the pencil lead.

3. Rest the lead on the cardboard, and place the batteries with opposite terminals together. Join a piece of wire to a paper clip, and attach it to the other end of the batteries.

2

3

WHY IT WORKS

A pencil lead is made of carbon, which conducts electricity. All conductors have some resistance which becomes higher the farther the electricity has to travel. As the paper clip moves toward the battery, the electricity doesn't have to travel as far. The bulb therefore becomes brighter. As it is moved away from the battery, the light dims.

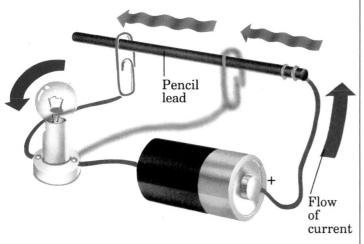

Pencil lead

Flow of current

BRIGHT IDEAS

Repeat the project attaching the paper clip to the wire from the bulb. Attach the pencil lead to the wire from the battery. When is the bulb brightest? Which way must you move the paper clip to dim the light now? Which works best?

Build a model theater set with a circuit of floor lights. Use colored paper to create colored lights. By building a variable resistor into the circuit you can dim or brighten the stage lights.

You can make another kind of dimmer by immersing a length of aluminum foil in salt water while it is connected to a circuit. A second piece of foil, connected to the other end of the circuit, is at the bottom of the container. Watch what happens when you move the top piece of foil up and down in the water.

6. Move the paper clip up and down the pencil lead. The bulb should get brighter or dimmer.

6

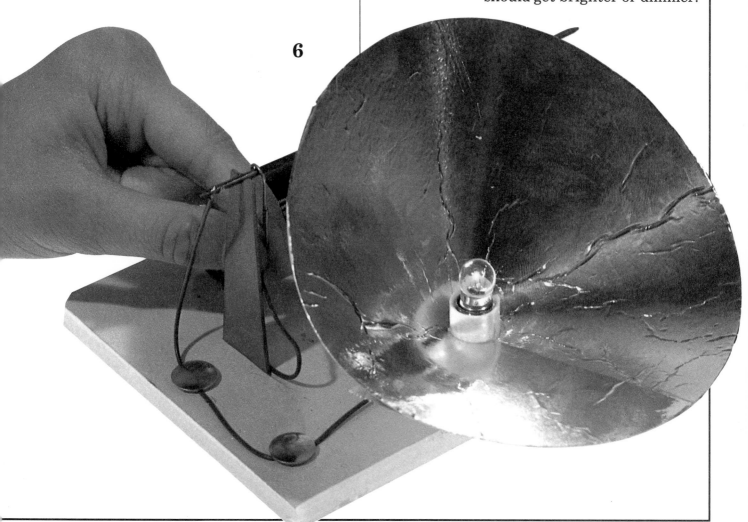

SERIES AND PARALLELS

As long ago as 1810, many larger cities had street lighting. An electric current was made to jump between two carbon rods – this was called electric arc lighting. First introduced by Sir Humphry Davy, these lamps were connected in series. This meant that all the lamps were connected as a part of one large circuit. It also meant that if one lamp went out, and the circuit was broken, they all went out. This often happens with Christmas tree lights, although they can be arranged in parallel circuits to avoid this problem. It was Thomas Edison who recognized the need to use parallel circuits for street lighting. Each bulb in a parallel circuit has a circuit of its own. If one bulb fails, the others will continue to glow; the current is divided equally between them.

LOTS OF LIGHTS

1

1. You will need two large boards, drawing pins, insulated wire, bulbs, bulb holders, and batteries. The drawing pins can act as contacts where your wires join.

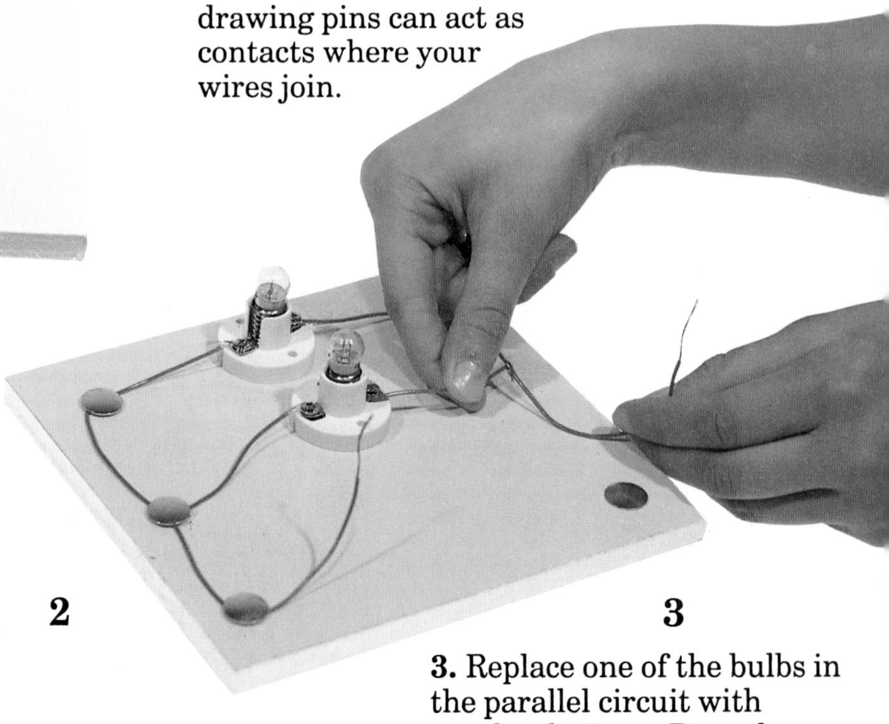

2. Set up your parallel circuit. If one bulb fails the other will remain lit because the circuits are separate. Observe how brightly the bulbs glow.

2

3

3. Replace one of the bulbs in the parallel circuit with another battery. Does the light from the bulb change? Now wire up a series circuit like the red one shown here. Include one bulb and two batteries in this circuit. Stop **immediately** if the batteries heat up.

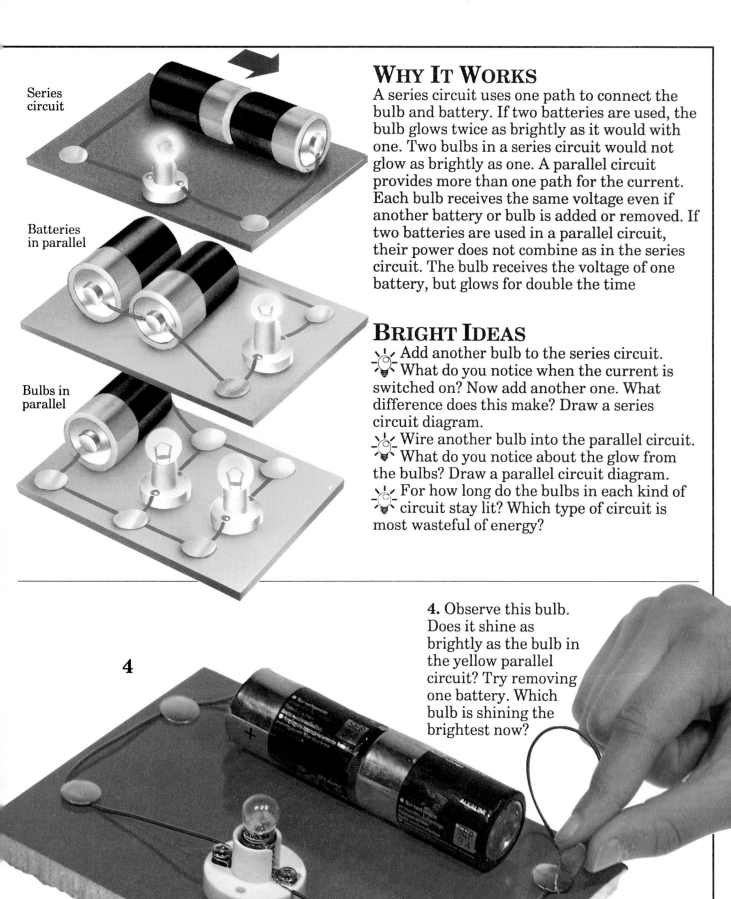

Series circuit

Batteries in parallel

Bulbs in parallel

WHY IT WORKS

A series circuit uses one path to connect the bulb and battery. If two batteries are used, the bulb glows twice as brightly as it would with one. Two bulbs in a series circuit would not glow as brightly as one. A parallel circuit provides more than one path for the current. Each bulb receives the same voltage even if another battery or bulb is added or removed. If two batteries are used in a parallel circuit, their power does not combine as in the series circuit. The bulb receives the voltage of one battery, but glows for double the time

BRIGHT IDEAS

Add another bulb to the series circuit. What do you notice when the current is switched on? Now add another one. What difference does this make? Draw a series circuit diagram.

Wire another bulb into the parallel circuit. What do you notice about the glow from the bulbs? Draw a parallel circuit diagram.

For how long do the bulbs in each kind of circuit stay lit? Which type of circuit is most wasteful of energy?

4. Observe this bulb. Does it shine as brightly as the bulb in the yellow parallel circuit? Try removing one battery. Which bulb is shining the brightest now?

4

71

ELECTRICITY IN THE HOME

Modern houses contain many electric circuits. Some circuits are for lighting and others power appliances or heaters. Access to the main circuit is made possible through wall sockets. All household lights and appliances are connected in parallel, as this allows all devices to operate on the same voltage. This voltage will not change if a piece of equipment is added or taken away (see page 70). The current leaves the house through another wire. Faulty wiring may cause a fire in the home. To avoid such a risk, plugs and circuits are fitted with fuses or circuit breakers. A fuse is a piece of wire designed to melt, and so break a circuit, if the current is too high. A complex circuit, like that in a television set, has hundreds or even thousands of circuit parts. They consist of both parallel and series circuits. Make your own game using circuits and switches.

TURN OFF THE LIGHT!

5. Now experiment with your circuit board. Can you light up only one bulb at a time by disconnecting certain switches? Now try lighting up two bulbs simultaneously. You can have hours of fun trying various connections. Observe the bulbs. When do they glow most brightly? When are they dimmest?

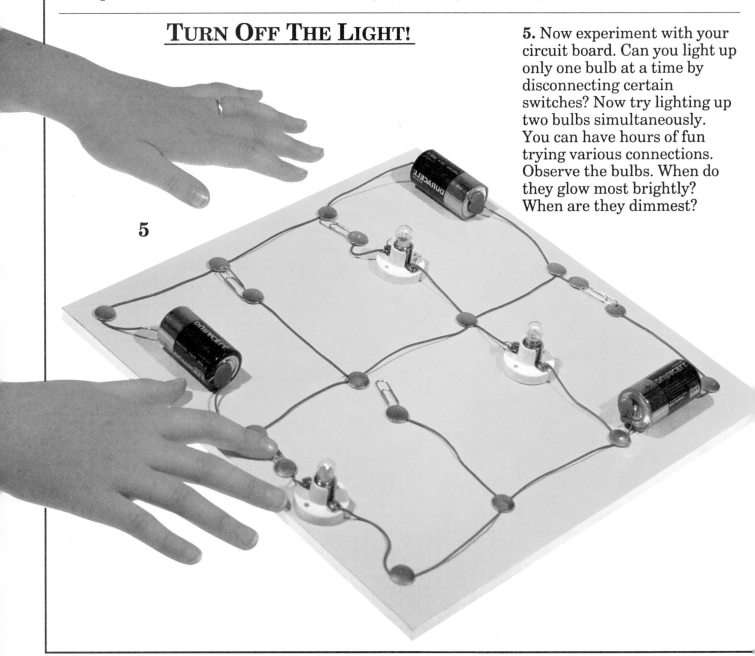

5

1. You will need a large board, three bulbs, three batteries, lengths of insulated wire, drawing pins, modeling clay, and paper clips.

WHY IT WORKS

The flow of electrons is regulated by connecting and disconnecting the switches on the circuit board. When a bulb is isolated by disconnecting a switch, the circuit into which it is wired is broken. When every switch is connected, all the bulbs glow. The high resistance of a fuse restricts the amount of current that can pass through. Each appliance needs a fuse of the correct resistance (see page 68).

2. Place a battery in three corners of the board. Make sure that unlike terminals are facing. Attach the wires using modeling clay.

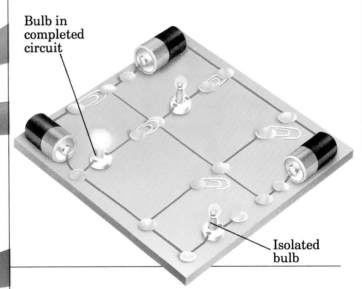

Bulb in completed circuit

Isolated bulb

3. Connect the bulbs to the batteries as shown. Leave gaps in the circuits for switches. These can be paper clips and drawing pins.

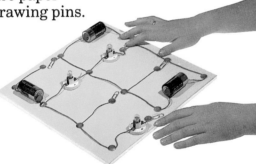

BRIGHT IDEAS

Position the batteries so that like terminals are facing each other. What effect does this have on your circuit board? Can the bulbs be lit up simultaneously now? Why is this? Remember that electrons travel from negative to positive. Do the bulbs glow just as brightly as before?

If you remove one bulb, how does this affect the circuits?

Ask an adult to show you where the electricity meter is located in your house. Keep a record of meter readings in your home for a week. Figure out how much electricity has been used. Use your figures to make a graph. You could put the information on a computer database if you have one at home or school. Count the number of sockets in your home. Make a list of all the electrical appliances used by your family. Watch the meter dials when each appliance is being used; which uses the most electricity? Figure out some ways in which your family could save electricity.

4. Connect each switch by pressing down a paper clip on to a drawing pin. Observe the brightness of the bulbs. If any of the bulbs do not work, check all connections.

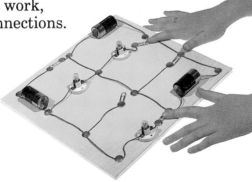

ELECTROMAGNETISM

The English physicist, Michael Faraday, discovered that electrical energy could be turned into mechanical energy (movement) by using magnetism. He used a cylindrical coil of wire, called a solenoid, to create a simple electric motor. He went on to discover that mechanical energy can be converted into electrical energy – the reverse of the principle of the electric motor. His work led to the development of the dynamo, or generator. You can make a powerful electromagnet by passing electricity through a coil of wire wrapped many times around a nail. Electromagnets are found in many everyday machines and gadgets. An MRI scanner (Magnetic Resonance Imaging), like the one pictured here, contains many ring-shaped electromagnets. With a solenoid and a current of electricity, you can close the cage.

CAGED!

1. Take a piece of polystyrene and edge it with cardboard. Stick plastic straws upright around three sides as the bars of the cage.

2. Cut out another piece of polystrene of the same size for the roof of the cage. Attach a piece of plastic straw to the side above the door. Wind a piece of wire around a nail 50 times leaving two ends. Affix the nail to the roof, as shown.

3. Insert a needle into the straw so that it almost touches the nail. Cut out a rectangle of plastic for the door. Make a hole at the bottom of the door for the needle to fit through.

4. Stick a piece of cardboard across the door to help hold it open, and make sure the end of the needle just pokes through the hole. Now attach one of the wires to one terminal on the battery. Leave the other free. Make sure it will reach the other terminal. Put the animal into the cage.

WHY IT WORKS

When the current is switched on, the nail becomes magnetized as the current flows through the wire. The needle in the door of the cage is attracted to the electromagnet. As the needle is pulled toward the nail, the door closes to trap the tiger.

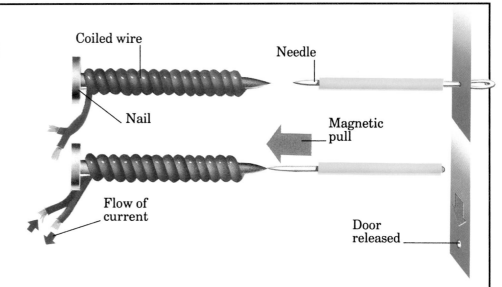

Coiled wire

Needle

Nail

Magnetic pull

Flow of current

Door released

BRIGHT IDEAS

💡 Wind more turns of wire onto the electromagnet. The magnetic effect will increase. What happens if you use a more powerful battery? (Do not let it get too hot.)

💡 Make another electromagnet using a shorter nail. This will also make the magnetic pull stronger.

💡 Make an electromagnetic pickup by winding wire around a nail. What objects can you pick up? What happens when the current is turned off?

💡 Use an electromagnet to make a carousel spin. Attach paper clips around the edge of a circular cardboard lid to be the roof. Make sure it is free to spin, and place an electromagnet close to the paper clips. The carousel should turn as you switch the current on and off quickly.

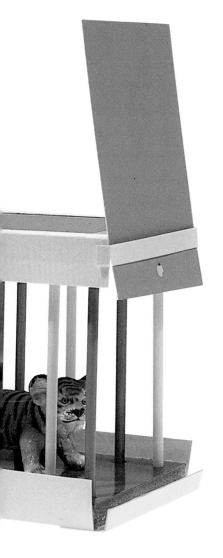

5. Now pick up the free wire. Allow the free wire to come into contact with the unconnected battery terminal. The needle should be pulled back toward the nail. The door will fall down, trapping the animal in its cage.

ELECTROLYSIS

Electrolysis is a process in which an electric current is passed through a liquid, causing a chemical reaction to take place. The liquid used is called the electrolyte. The wires or plates where the current enters or leaves the liquid are called electrodes. The electrolysis of metallic solutions is useful in putting metal coatings on objects. If you have a look at some car bumpers, you will notice that they may have a nice, smooth, metallic appearance. This is because they are coated with a metal called nickel, in a process called electroplating. This helps to stop the metal underneath from rusting. The same method is used to coat cutlery with silver. This is called silverplating. Michael Faraday discovered the first law of electrolysis. The process is also used to purify metals like aluminum.

COPPER PLATING

1. For this project you will need a glass jar, a copper coin, a paper clip, two batteries, insulated wire, and water. Pour the water into the jar. Place the batteries together with unlike terminals adjacent. Connect wires to the terminals. Attach the copper to the wire from the positive terminal of the battery. The paper clip must be attached to the wire from the negative terminal. Use modeling clay. Do not allow the metal objects to touch in the solution. You could even tape each wire to the side of the jar so that they are suspended.

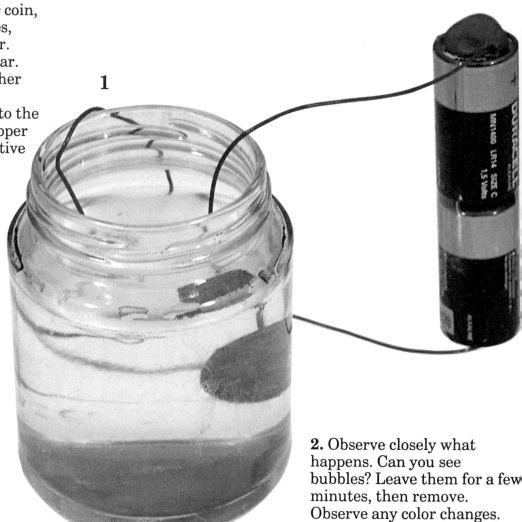

1

2. Observe closely what happens. Can you see bubbles? Leave them for a few minutes, then remove. Observe any color changes. Replace them for a while. Are there any further changes?

WHY IT WORKS

The copper coin is connected to the positive terminal of the battery – the current enters here. The other, the paper clip, is joined to the negative terminal – the current leaves here. As the current flows through the water from the positive electrode (anode) to the negative electrode (cathode), the copper is carried from the coin to the clip.

Movement of copper

BRIGHT IDEAS

Repeat the project using salt dissolved in vinegar instead of the water. What difference do you notice – if any? What do you observe about the appearance of the paper clip? Maybe your school has scales that can weigh very small objects? If the coin and the paper clip are weighed before immersion in the liquid and their weight recorded, you can check whether electroplating has really taken place. After carrying out the project weigh them both again. Now replace the battery with a more powerful one, or add a second battery into a parallel circuit, to increase the "push" of the current passing through the liquid. (Remember to stop your experiments if the batteries heat up.) Weigh the coin and paper clip a second time. If the weight of the paper clip has increased further, then you have proved the first law of electrolysis – the size of the charge passed through the liquid determines the amount of copper freed.

2

MAGNETISM

INTRODUCTION

Magnetism is a force that acts between magnets. You may think of magnets as toys that pick up nails or other bits of iron and steel, but magnetism is an important force in nature. Magnetism is all around us and we use it every day. Magnets come in all shapes and sizes. Magnets are used in telephones, television sets, and radios; they can work giant machines, they can seek out North in direction, and they can push and pull other magnets. In fact, the world has become a different place since magnetism was first discovered. People once believed that magnets had mystical powers and could heal the sick. It was when sailors first learned how to magnetize a compass needle, however, that the age of science began. The Magnetic North Pole of the earth was located in 1831 by Sir James Clark Ross, and almost 100 years later, in 1909, the Magnetic South Pole was located by a party led by Lord Shackleton. Today, we know much more about the Earth and magnetism. We even rely on magnetism to produce large amounts of electricity for us. As you find out more about magnetism and magnets, you will discover that they are not only very useful, but a great deal of fun too!

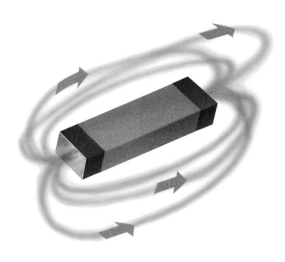

Magnetic Attraction

Archaeologists and beachcombers often make use of metal detectors to locate buried objects or treasure. Materials are either magnetic or nonmagnetic. Most, but not all, metals are magnetic. Iron has the strongest magnetic attraction. Nickel and cobalt are also magnetic, as are the alloys, or mixtures, of these metals. Aluminum, copper, and gold are nonmagnetic. Magnetic ferrites (metals containing iron) can be used to make hard magnets, like the refrigerator magnets pictured here. These are known as permanent magnets. Soft magnets are temporary and are easy to magnetize and demagnetize. Magnetic materials can be easily separated from other materials. When aluminum cans are recycled, they are sorted from other metals by using a magnet. You can make your own metal detector with an ordinary magnet. See if you can find any buried treasure!

Secrets In The Sand

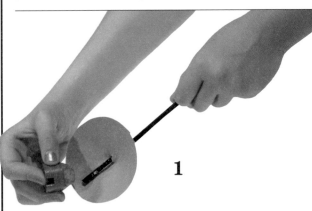

1

2 Hold the cone in place by attaching small strips of paper to it and winding them tightly around the stick. Now decorate the cone with paint or colored paper.

2

1 Make a circle, 4 inches across out of colored cardboard and cut a slit from the edge to the center. Overlap the two ends and glue, to create a flat cone. Push one end of a stick through the center and attach a button magnet to the stick with clay.

3 Half fill a shallow container with clean sand. Bury a variety of objects in the sand, metals and nonmetals.

4 Move your metal detector slowly above the surface of the sand. Try it at various heights. You will soon discover how low you must hold it to attract objects.

3

WHY IT WORKS

A magnet exerts a force on a nearby piece of magnetic material by turning it into a weak magnet – this is magnetic induction. A magnet is made up of many tiny parts called domains. Each one is like a mini-magnet, and they all point in the same direction. The domains in a metal are jumbled up. When a magnet comes into contact with the metal, the domains line up and the metal becomes magnetized. A strong magnet can act over quite a distance. Each object picked up from the sand is a temporary magnet because the domains inside become aligned.

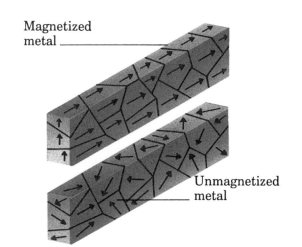

Magnetized metal

Unmagnetized metal

BRIGHT IDEAS

🔆 Predict which objects you expect your magnet to pick up - you may be surprised! See how near to the sand the magnet must be held before it picks anything up. At what height does it fail to attract any of the hidden objects? Keep a record of your results.

🔆 Which objects does your magnet pick up? Which are left buried in the sand? What does this tell you about them? (Hint: the answer is on this page.) Notice whether any of the magnetic objects keep their magnetism and attract other objects.

🔆 Try a different kind of magnet. See if you can pick up any more objects with it. See what happens if you add more sand to the container.

🔆 Find out which other metals are non-magnetic. Collect some empty drink cans and sort them with a magnet. Remember, aluminum is nonmagnetic. Save the cans for recycling.

4

WHERE IS MAGNETISM?

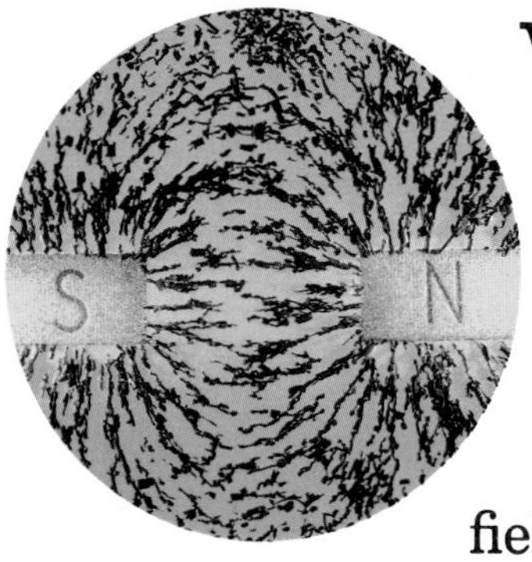

Magnetite, or lodestone, is a naturally occurring magnetic ferrite. The first magnets were made by stroking magnetic materials with a lodestone. You will find magnets of many shapes and sizes – bar, horseshoe, and button are only a few. Every magnet is surrounded by something called a magnetic field, wherever magnetism is found. The areas of the magnet where magnetism is at its strongest are called the poles. Every magnet has at least two poles. Poles are named after the direction they point in. These are North and South.

Iron filings

FLAT FIELDS

1 Place two bar magnets beneath a large sheet of paper, resting each end of the paper on a thin book. Position the magnets with unlike poles facing each other.

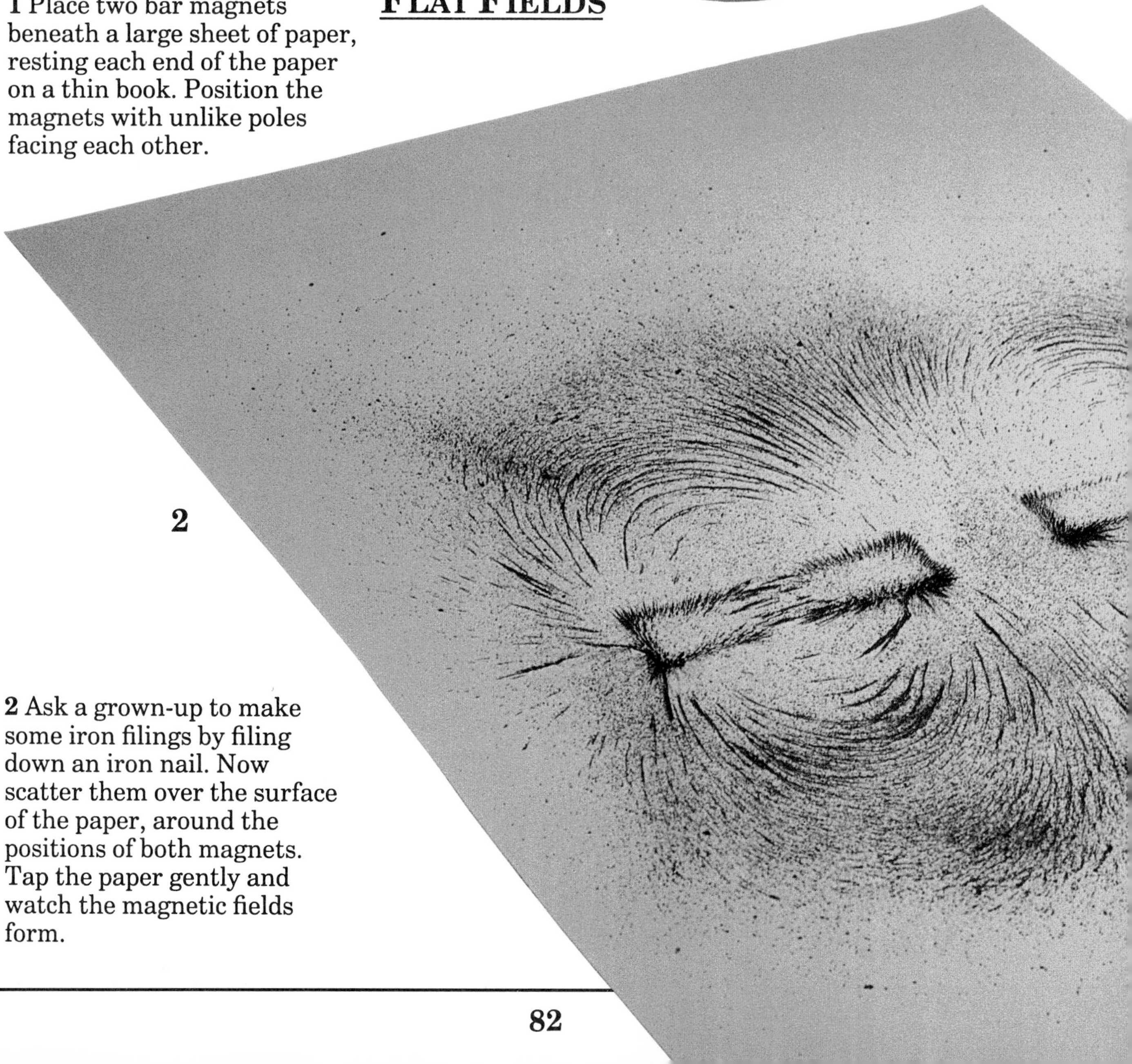

2

2 Ask a grown-up to make some iron filings by filing down an iron nail. Now scatter them over the surface of the paper, around the positions of both magnets. Tap the paper gently and watch the magnetic fields form.

WHY IT WORKS

Magnetic lines of force run from north to south and they are strongest where the lines are closest together. This indicates where the poles of the magnet are located. Because like poles repel, for example two south poles, the magnetic fields of the magnets also repel each other. As the iron filings are magnetized they are drawn into the magnetic field, showing the lines of force around the magnet.

BRIGHT IDEAS

Move the two magnets so that like poles are facing each other. Notice that the shape of the magnetic field has changed.

Repeat the experiment with magnets of different shapes and observe the pattern of the magnetic field of each.

Hit a magnet with a hammer – notice what effect this has on the magnet. See if you can still show its magnetic field with the iron filings.

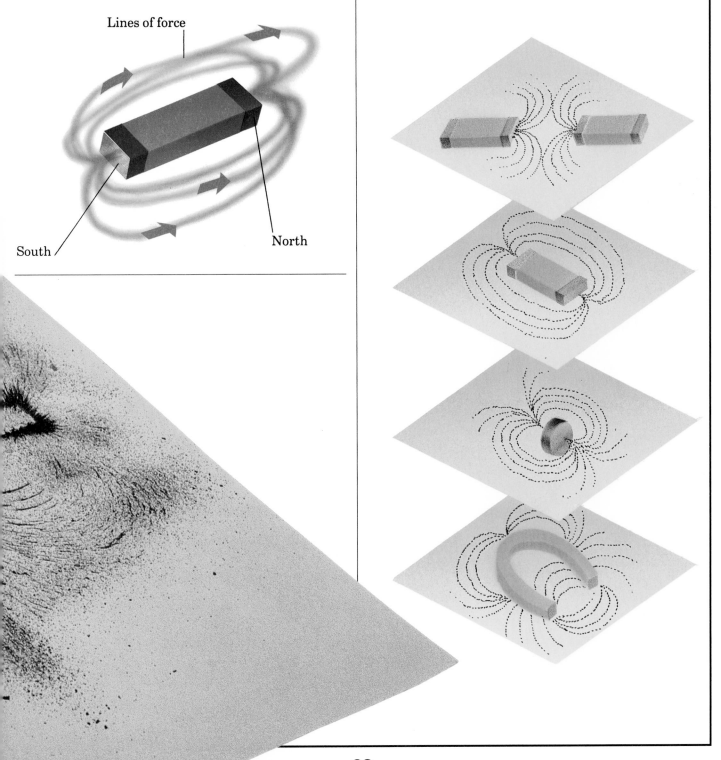

Lines of force

South

North

MAGNETIC FIELDS

The space around a permanent magnet in which its effects can be felt is called its magnetic field. A permanent magnet exerts a force that extends some distance from it in every direction. These invisible lines are like closed loops, with part of the loop inside the magnet and part forming the field outside. The lines of force never touch or cross. You have already seen how iron filings give a flat picture of a magnetic field. A magnetic field can cause a compass needle, which is itself a bar magnet, to move. The presence of a magnet near electrical equipment can create havoc, in the same way as the magnetic needle in a compass is made to move. Magnetic shields are designed to avoid such problems (see page 88). Using iron filings and oil you can demonstrate the three-dimensional nature of a magnetic field.

OIL FIELDS

1 Fill a see-through container almost to the top with a clear, thick liquid like cooking oil or glycerine. Scatter iron filings into the liquid and gently stir the mixture with a stick to disperse the filings evenly.

1

2 Now place a bar magnet underneath the jar and allow the filings to settle. View them from above. You will see the magnetic field of the magnet as a three-dimensional pattern formed by the iron filings.

BRIGHT IDEAS

Try holding a horseshoe magnet against the outside of the jar. See what effect this has on the iron filings in the oil. Notice where the lines of force are closest together.

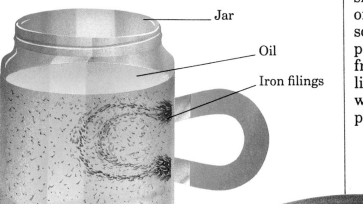

Jar

Oil

Iron filings

WHY IT WORKS

The iron filings become temporary magnets while inside the magnetic field of the bar magnet, bunching together where the field is strongest. The oil supports the filings in the shape they form around the magnet. The lines of force in a magnetic field move from north to south. Every magnet has a North and South pole at each end, like the Earth. As you can see from the shape appearing in the oil, magnetic lines of force are closest at the poles – this is where the magnet is strongest. The weakest part of a magnet is at its center.

2

ATTRACTION AND REPULSION

Within its magnetic field a magnet will either attract or repel another magnet. If two metal objects attract each other, it is difficult to tell which one is the magnet. The only true test of a magnet is to see if it is repelled by another magnet. A bar magnet has two poles, one North and one South. If a bar magnet is broken in the middle, new poles will appear at the broken ends. As we know that like poles repel and unlike poles attract, it is wrong to describe the North-seeking point of a compass needle as "North." In fact, it is the South pole of the magnetic needle that is attracted to the earth's magnetic North Pole. Always use the term "North-seeking" to avoid confusion. Using the laws of magnetic attraction and repulsion, see if you can move a toy car around the track. The attraction and repulsion between the two magnets should be strong enough to push and pull the car. Maybe you can win a race!

TRACK EVENT

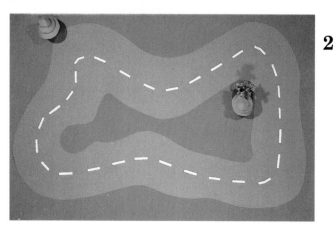

1

1 Firmly attach a bar magnet to the roof of a toy car. Use some strong tape. Make sure that the magnet is well balanced.

2 Cut out a racetrack from gray cardboard and attach it with glue to a sheet of green cardboard – make sure there are no bumps. Add some trees.

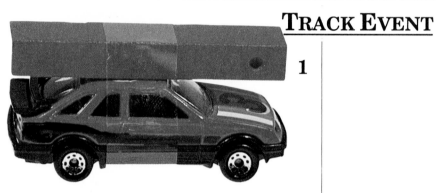

2

3 Place the car on the track. Hold one end of a bar magnet close to the end of the magnet at the rear of the car. If the car moves backward turn the magnet you are holding around the other way. You can push or pull the car around the track by holding the magnet in different places.

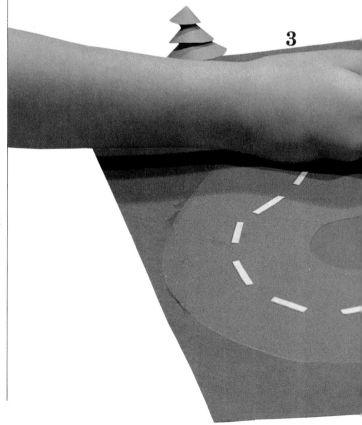

3

WHY IT WORKS

Magnets can push or pull because like poles repel but unlike poles attract. This attraction and repulsion is strong enough to push and pull the car around the track.

When two north poles face each other the opposing magnetic fields cancel each other out – this is called the neutral point. The repulsion between two like poles can be so strong that it is impossible to push them together. This magnetic force can be used to push the toy car around the track. In the same way, the attraction between opposite poles can be used to drag the car along.

BRIGHT IDEAS

Suspend a small magnet above a needle attached by thread to a flat surface. Watch the needle rise up into the air.

Suspend a bar magnet freely. Close to it suspend a second magnet. Watch them move as the like poles pull away from each other.

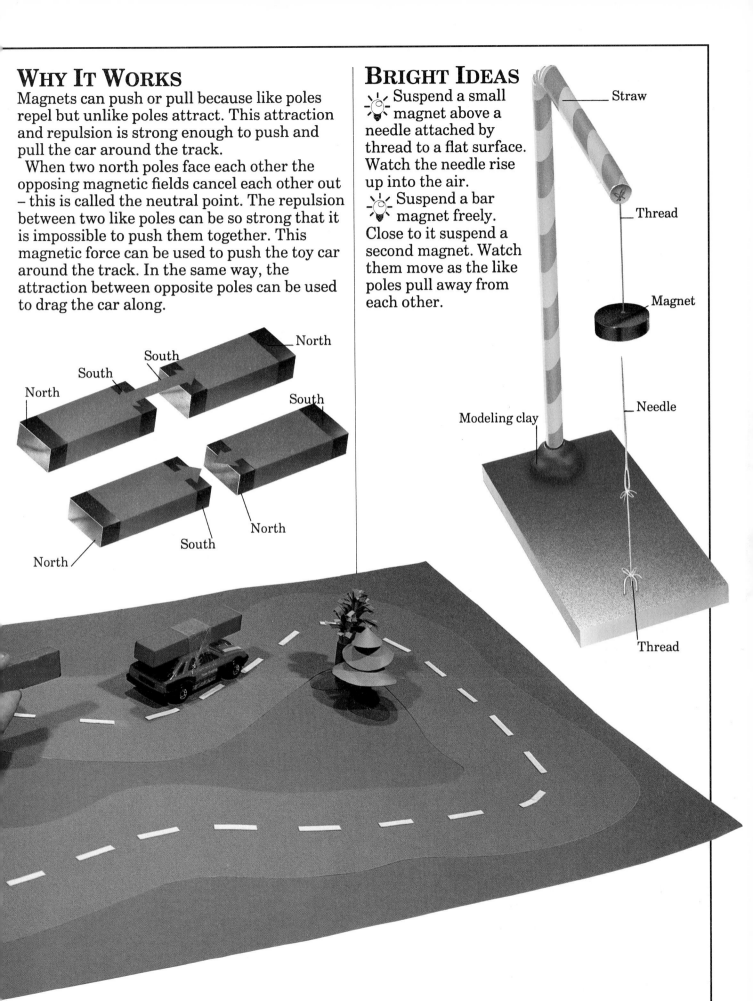

North
South
South
North
North
South
South
North

Straw
Thread
Magnet
Needle
Modeling clay
Thread

MAGNETISM TRAVELS

A magnetic force can travel through many substances. It can even travel through water. Treasure on the seabed can be detected by a diver carrying an instrument called a magnetometer. The same is true of other nonmagnetic materials – you have already seen how magnetic lines of force can travel through paper to the iron filings. What other materials do you think magnetism could travel through? Because tiny magnets as fine as powder are used to store images and sounds on tapes and computer disks, a magnetic field can interfere with the quality. The effect can only be lessened by placing another magnetic object within the magnetic field. This is a shield that cancels out the effect. Make this hockey game and prove that magnetism can travel through nonmagnetic materials.

1 Cut out two figures holding hockey sticks from cardboard. Color them so that they are wearing different shirts. Behind each hockey stick attach a small magnet with modeling clay.

FACE-OFF!

2 Attach a bar magnet firmly to one end of two long sticks. These sticks can then be held underneath the "rink" and used to move the players.

3 The hockey rink can be made from a painted cardboard lid raised up on four wooden legs. Fold two strips of cardboard to be the goalposts. Mark the center line and circles with colored tape. Put the "players" in position, facing each other. You can score goals using a Ping-Pong ball.

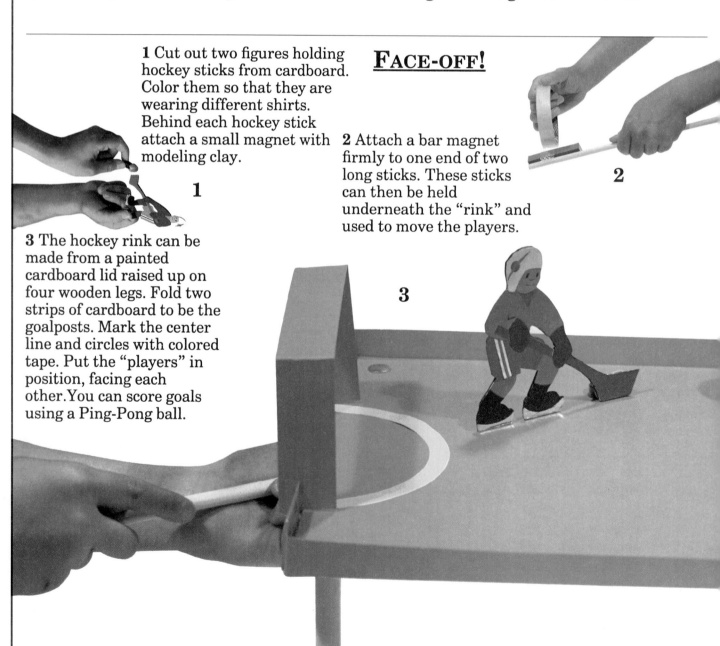

WHY IT WORKS

Nonmagnetic materials allow a magnetic field to pass through them. A magnetic material will pick up the magnetic force and weaken it. Cardboard is not magnetic. It allows a magnetic force to pass through it. Distance is important. If the magnet is too far away or if the nonmagnetic material is too thick, the effect of the magnet will not be felt. Some magnets are stronger than others. The weaker the magnet, the closer it must be held to the magnetic material. A strong magnet can be held further away because its magnetic field is larger.

BRIGHT IDEAS

Fill a plastic see-through container with water and attach a paper clip to the bottom with modeling clay, as shown. Now take a cork and insert another paper clip to make a hook. Using a bar magnet on the outside of the container, see if you can drag the cork to the bottom and anchor it to the clip. See what other materials magnetism will work through. Try plastic, wood, and china.

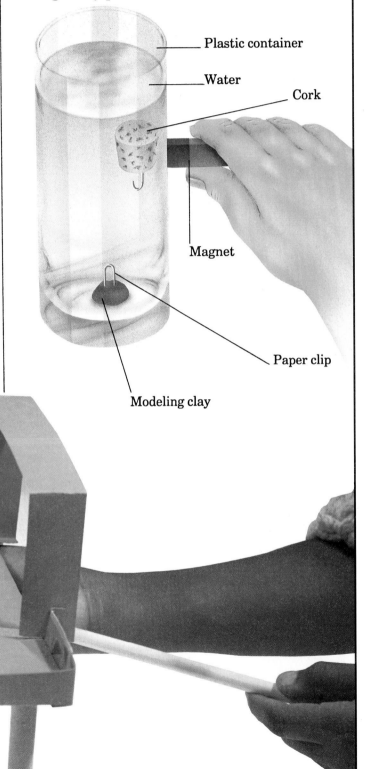

Plastic container

Water

Cork

Magnet

Paper clip

Modeling clay

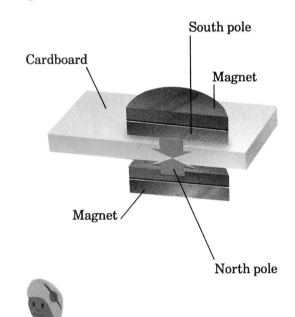

South pole

Magnet

Cardboard

Magnet

North pole

THE EARTH IS A MAGNET

As long ago as 1600, William Gilbert noted that a round lodestone showed all the magnetic properties of the Earth in miniature. He called it a "terella," meaning "little Earth." The inside of the earth behaves like a massive magnet. Imagine a giant bar magnet at its center. A compass needle points to the magnetic North Pole, not true north. When orienteering (mapreading), always allow for the difference between the two by lining up north on the map with north on the compass. Migrating birds are thought to use the Earth's magnetic field to navigate. Racing pigeons are known to fly off course during a magnetic storm, when changes occur in the Earth's magnetic field. The Northern and Southern lights are an impressive sight at the Poles. They are caused by the collision of solar winds with the Earth's magnetic field.

SEEKING NORTH!

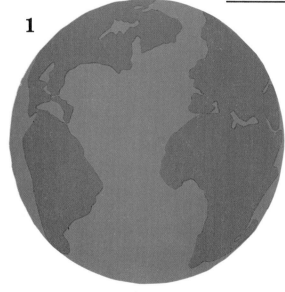

1

1 Cut out a circle of blue cardboard and trace the map of the world onto cardboard of another color. Now stick this down to represent the Earth.

2 You will need five compasses to lay around the outside of your map.

2

3

3 Lay the bar magnet under your map, with the North pole at the top and South pole at the bottom.

WHY IT WORKS

The north-seeking poles of the compasses follow the magnetic lines of force of the bar magnet, not those of the real Earth. A similar field, however, lies around the earth. At the top half of your map, the north-seeking pole of the compasses points to the north pole of the magnet and the miniature Earth. At the bottom half of the map, the south-seeking pole points to the south pole of the map. Lines of force span the Earth from pole to pole.

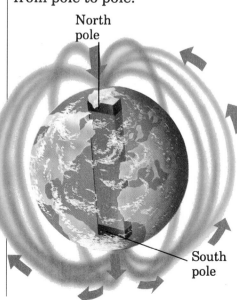

North pole

South pole

90

BRIGHT IDEAS

Place a compass on top of a map of your locality. Establish where magnetic north is, then rotate the map until north on the map is lined up with the north-seeking point of the compass needle. This is called orienting a map. In which direction are east, south, and west in relation to north?

North-seeking point

Compass

North

South

Magnet

South-seeking point

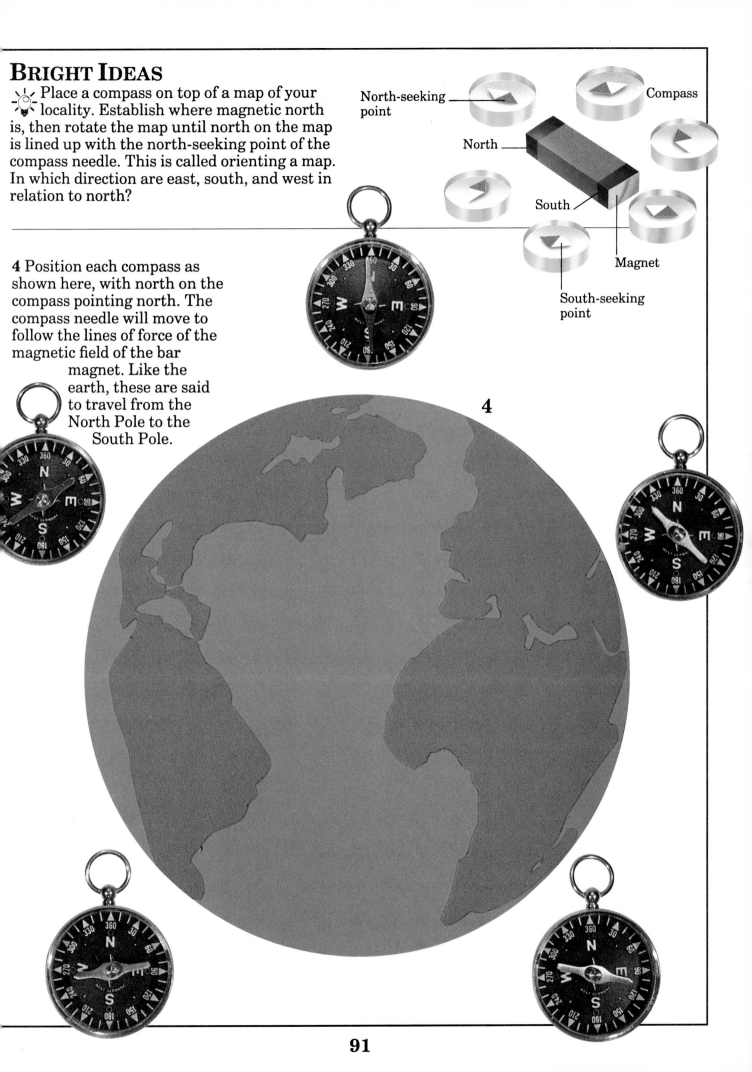

4 Position each compass as shown here, with north on the compass pointing north. The compass needle will move to follow the lines of force of the magnetic field of the bar magnet. Like the earth, these are said to travel from the North Pole to the South Pole.

4

FOLLOWING MAGNETS

Almost 2,000 years ago, the Chinese knew how to make a simple compass by suspending a long, thin piece of magnetite or lodestone. Later, sailors used a lodestone to magnetize the needle for a ship's compass. Compasses were being used in China in the eleventh century. The Italian explorer, Amerigo Vespucci, whose name was mistakenly given to America, understood the concept of a magnetic North Pole. It was not until the sixteenth century, however, that it was fully accepted. Christopher Columbus was unable to navigate with total accuracy, because his compass readings were inaccurate – probably due to magnetic interference. Today, many large ships have a gyrocompass. This gives a bearing (compass direction) in relation to true north. Make your own simple compass by magnetizing a needle.

CRAFT A COMPASS

1 You will need a waterproof plate, a cork, a magnet, and a steel needle. Half fill the plate with clean water. Holding the magnet the same way all the time, stroke the needle with it at least 50 times. Always stroke in the same direction and lift the magnet off the needle each time you want to begin another stroke.

2 The needle has now been magnetized permanently, because it is steel. Push it through the cork so that the cork balances on the water evenly. Allow the water to become absolutely still. The needle will seek out the earth's magnetic North Pole to point north. Make sure there are no magnetic materials nearby.

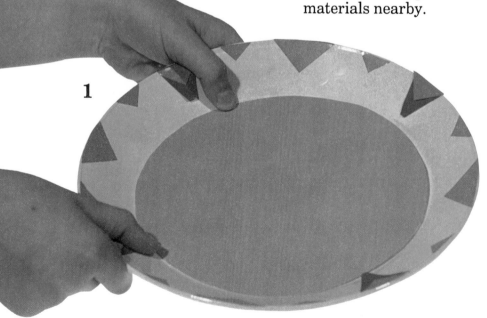

WHY IT WORKS

By stroking a permanent magnet along the needle, the domains inside become aligned. This turns the needle into a magnet, too. Any magnet free to turn horizontally will settle pointing north/south, as the north-seeking pole is attracted to the earth's magnetic North Pole.

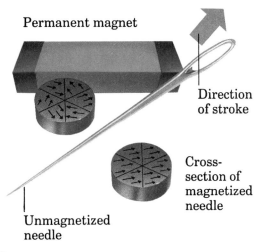

Permanent magnet

Direction of stroke

Cross-section of magnetized needle

Unmagnetized needle

BRIGHT IDEAS

☀ Find a way to mark your compass clearly with the four compass directions. You could even design a compass rose.

☀ Make a different kind of compass by pivoting a magnetized needle on folded cardboard on top of a stick. The stick is kept upright inside a container using modeling clay.

☀ Place a paper clip underneath a metal lid made from a magnetic metal. Try to move the paper clip from beneath the lid with a magnet. You will find it difficult. Why is this?

☀ Using a bar magnet you can show how a compass needle seeks out north. Suspend the magnet freely - make sure there are no magnets nearby - the magnet will rotate until it points north-south. The north-seeking pole (which is the south pole of the magnet) will face north.

☀ Try floating a bar magnet on wood or cork in a bowl of water. What do you expect to happen?

☀ Draw an eight-point compass. What is the size of the angle between each compass point?

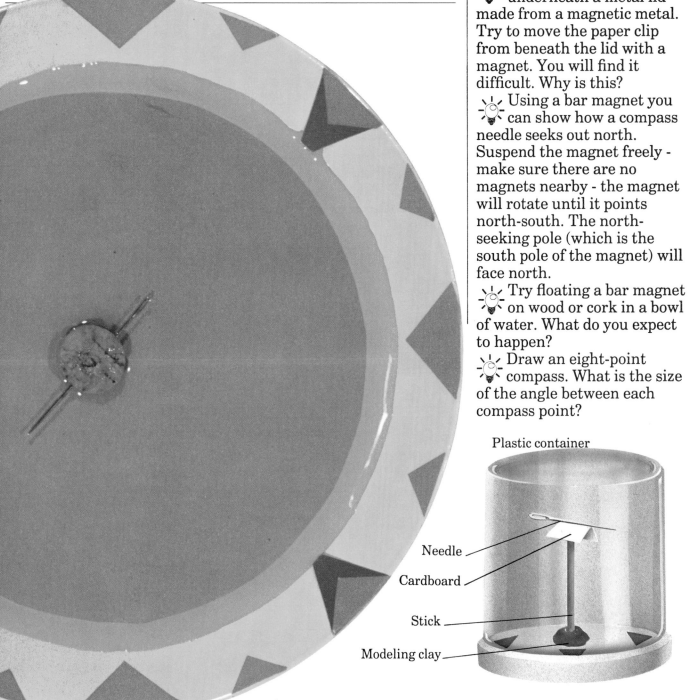

Plastic container

Needle

Cardboard

Stick

Modeling clay

93

ELECTROMAGNETS

The discovery of electromagnets in the 1800s was the first step in investigating the relationship between electricity and magnetism. In 1820, a Danish physicist, Hans Christian Oersted, discovered that a wire conducting an electric current produces a surrounding magnetic field. We now know that when electricity flows through a coil of wire wrapped around a soft iron core it creates a strong magnet, called an electromagnet. Electromagnets are used in many appliances and machines. Doorbells, telephones, and burglar alarms are only a few. The most powerful electromagnets are those used in scrapyards to lift heavy pieces of metal. You can build your own pickup using an electromagnet.

A MAGNETIC PICKUP

1 Use two boxes to make the crane. Make the arm from cardboard, using a thread spool and pencil to create a lever. Wind insulated wire (blue) around an iron nail 50 times.

2 Take one end of the blue wire to the battery in the base and the other to a drawing pin in the side of the body. Attach a paper clip to this pin to create a switch (as shown), and insert another pin within reach of the clip.

3 To this second pin attach the red wire, taking the other end to the battery. When the paper clip joins both drawing pins, electricity flows through the wires causing the nail to become magnetized.

Flow
of
electricity

Magnetized
nail

Wire

Unmagnetized
nail

Domains

WHY IT WORKS

An electromagnet is a coil of wire around an iron core. When an electric current flows through the coil a strong magnetic field is created. The strength of the field depends upon the "push" of the current – the voltage. The strength of an electromagnet can be increased by the addition of extra turns of wire to the coil, by increasing the voltage in the circuit and by bringing the poles of the magnet closer together. If steel and not iron is used the metal will stay permanently magnetized. Iron becomes a temporary magnet. This means that when the current is switched off, the magnetic field disappears.

BRIGHT IDEAS

Wind about 60 turns of insulated wire around a steel nail. Connect the end to the battery and turn on the power. You have made a magnet. Make extra turns in the wire around the nail. Add another battery to the circuit. Observe any changes.

MAGNETS & MOVEMENT

Electric motors use magnets to turn electricity into movement. In 1821 Michael Faraday developed the electric motor. He discovered that continuous motion could be produced by passing an electric current through a conductor in a strong magnetic field. Electrical appliances like washing machines and vacuum cleaners have electric motors. The TGV, one of France's most powerful trains, is powered by electric motors. An electric motor is a coil turning between the two poles of a permanent magnet. When current flows through the coil, a magnetic field is produced that turns the rotor. This movement is converted into electricity. A generator that powers bicycle lights (right) works on this principle.

SPIN THE COMPASS

1 Position two batteries with opposite terminals touching and hold them in place with paper and tape.

2 Wind a long length of insulated wire around a cardboard core at least 50 times – this could be a slice of cardboard tube. Leave two ends free to connect to the battery.

3 Attach the coil of wire to the base with tape. You have made a solenoid. Also attach the batteries.

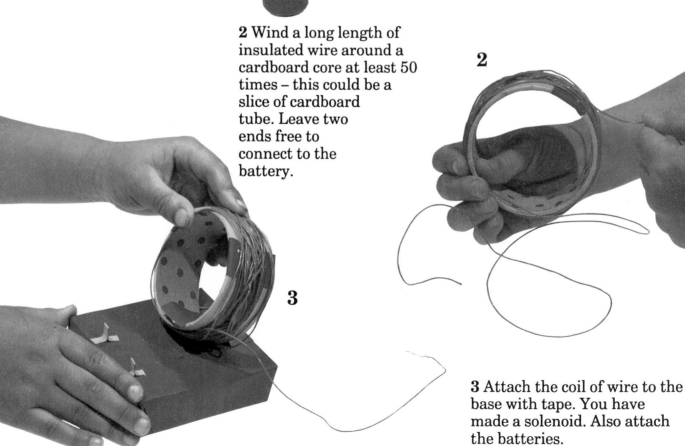

WHY IT WORKS

The magnetic field created by the electric current through the coil is strong enough to move the compass needle. When the current is turned on and off rapidly, the compass needle spins around continuously. The wire is copper. It is not magnetic and it does not affect the compass. When the electricity is turned on, each turn of wire has its own magnetic field. It is called a solenoid. A simple electric motor is a coil of wire mounted on a rod, so that it can rotate in a magnetic field. A current is passed into and out of the coil. An electric motor is clean and quiet.

BRIGHT IDEAS

-ஜ்- A simple electric motor like the one pictured here can be found in toy cars, hair dryers, and power drills. Maybe you could open up a broken toy and have a look?

-ஜ்- Recreate Faraday's experiment to illustrate the reverse principle - how a magnet can induce an electric current. You will need a small compass, placed inside a box. Wind at least 20 turns of wire around the box; at the other end of the wire you need a coil of at least 50 turns. Slowly pass a bar magnet through the coil and observe the compass.

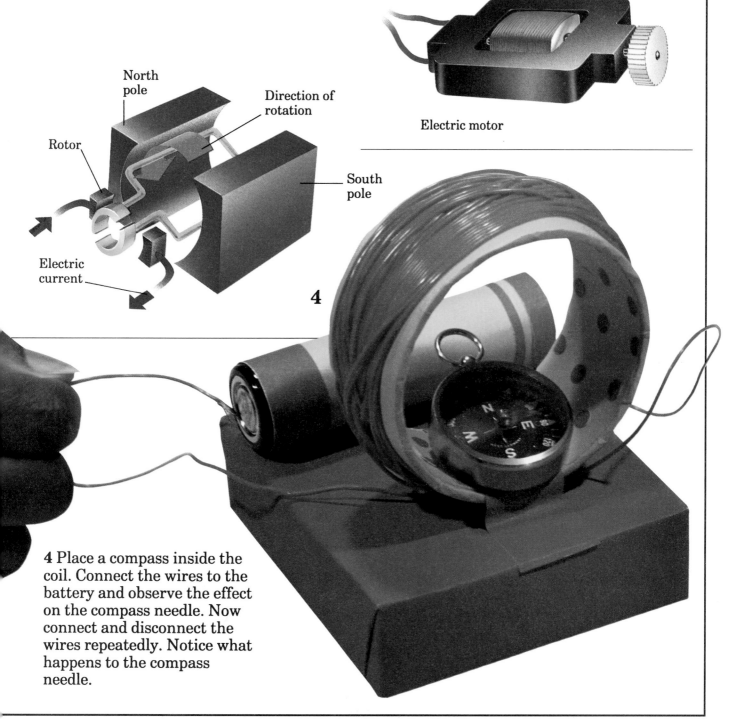

Electric motor

4 Place a compass inside the coil. Connect the wires to the battery and observe the effect on the compass needle. Now connect and disconnect the wires repeatedly. Notice what happens to the compass needle.

USING MAGNETISM

The magnets used by scientists vary in size, shape, and strength. With the development of electricity, the electromagnet is now part of much modern equipment, both scientific and domestic. Numerous gadgets and machines work for us because of magnetism. They range from a lid-holding can opener to an atom-smashing machine, called a particle accelerator. In our homes, weak magnets help to hold refrigerator doors firmly shut. In factories, magnetic conveyor belts transport iron and steel cans. Precision instruments may have lightweight moving parts suspended inside them with a magnet. We all make use of machines like the ticket machines pictured here. They can sort coins into their different values. You can also sort coins using your own magnetic slot machine.

A MAGNETIC SLOT MACHINE

1

1 Take a piece of stiff cardboard and attach a strong magnet underneath with tape. Attach it to the left side of the piece of cardboard.

2 Now fit the cardboard diagonally inside a tall box as shown. Hinge one side of the box to allow access.

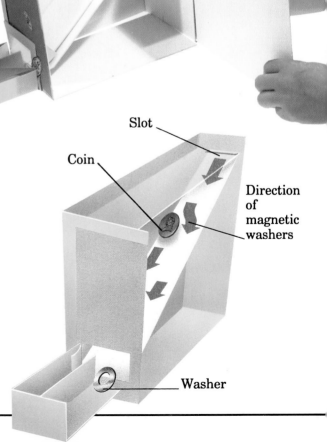

2

Slot

Coin

Direction of magnetic washers

Washer

WHY IT WORKS

When you drop the coins and washers into the slot, they travel down the shute, passing over the magnet. The metal washers, which are magnetic, are diverted by the magnetic field and fall into the left-hand compartment. The coins, which are not magnetic, carry on straight down the chute landing in the right-hand compartment. A real vending machine tests the coins with an electric current. It can sort the coins by testing the amount of electricity conducted.

Bright Ideas

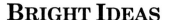

☀ If you push the "coins" through the slot with greater force does it make any difference? Examine your results and draw conclusions from them.

☀ With small button magnets you can make some magnetic stickers. Cut out letters or shapes and color them in. Use them to make a board game.

☀ Draw your own weather map on magnetic material and design some weather symbols that can be mounted on small magnets.

3 Cut an opening at the bottom of the box, the same width as the stiff cardboard. Attach a cardboard tray divided into sections, as shown. Enclose the top of the box, cutting a slit adjacent to the top of the stiff, sloping cardboard. Make the slit long enough to allow coins to be pushed through.

4 Finish off your machine by decorating the outside. Collect as many different coins and metal washers as you can and roll each through the machine.

3

FLOATING MAGNETS

You have already learned that like poles repel and unlike poles attract. This principle has been adapted and used in industry and the world of transportation. In factories and other places where steel sheets need to be lifted, magnetic floaters, which are large permanent magnets, are placed on either side of steel sheets. They magnetize the steel and cause poles to form in adjacent parts of the sheets. As the like poles repel one another they cause the top sheet to lift off the pile. Electromagnets can create a moving magnetic field. The Maglev train (pictured above) works on this principle. The Maglev has no wheels – it is levitated along the track as two magnetic fields repel each other.

LEVITATION

1

3

2 The cutout magician is secured to a cardboard window that is the same size as the back of the box. Slide the magician inside the box so that he stands behind the magnet, touching it.

1 You will need a cardboard box wide enough to hold a bar magnet, two strong bar magnets, cardboard, and tape. Cut away one side of the box and fold back a second side to give access to the "stage." Attach two strips of cardboard to the floor wide enough to hold one of the bar magnets in place. Position the North pole of the magnet to the left side of the stage when you are facing it.

2

3 Cover the sides with fabric to look like curtains. To the second magnet attach a cardboard cutout "assistant," as shown. Ensure that the head of the figure is positioned at the North pole of the magnet.

WHY IT WORKS

Magnets can push as well as pull. The strongest part of a magnetic field is at the poles and like poles repel. As both ends of the magnets repel each other, the top magnet is able to float above the other. It is important to support the top magnet at the sides so it cannot be pushed off in one direction.

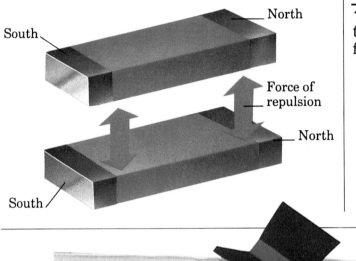

South

North

Force of repulsion

North

South

BRIGHT IDEAS

☀ Place some balsa wood between two magnets with opposite poles facing each other. Tape them together at each end and remove the wood. Press down on the top magnet. You will feel the "spring" of repulsion. This is how the Maglev train works.

☀ Get some small ring magnets and arrange them along a pencil. Place them so that they repel each other and see them float.

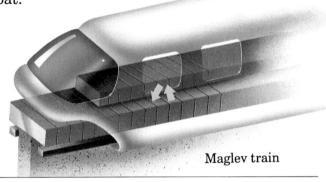

Maglev train

4

4 Place a small pencil or a piece of wood across the magnet on the floor of the stage. Gently position the "assistant" on top of it, parallel with the first magnet. Her head should be on the left. You may need to tape the ends of the two magnets together. Carefully remove the pencil and watch the lady levitate.

SOUND, NOISE AND MUSIC

INTRODUCTION

In science, sound is a form of energy, like light or heat. To us, though, it is many things. It can be the annoying noise of a barking dog, the beautiful music of an orchestra, or the soothing sound of waves on the shore. Sound can travel through most things, whether they are gas, liquid, or solid. However, it cannot travel through space. In air, sound travels out in all directions until it is interrupted by something solid. These solid objects reflect sound, causing echoes. Sounds are formed by vibrating objects. For example, your vocal chords when you sing, a guitar string when you pluck it, and a drum when you bang it, all have vibrating parts. These vibrations cause sound waves which travel through the air at about 1,100 feet per second to reach our ears. Some sounds are too high for people to hear, but can be picked up by many animals like bats or dogs. Some sounds are too low to hear, but we may still feel their vibrations. Babies still in the womb can hear sounds, whales in the sea can hear sounds carried through the water, and grasshoppers hear sounds through ears situated on their knees! People who cannot hear sounds may use special hearing aids to help them.

VIBRATIONS

Have you ever thrown a pebble into a pond and watched the ripples spread? The impact of the pebble in the water creates waves – and in a similar way all sounds cause waves in the air. Unlike water waves, sound waves do not move up and down, but travel forward in regions of high and low pressure. Sounds are produced by very fast back and forth movements called vibrations. If you hold your throat lightly a few inches below your chin and talk, you will feel the vibrations. These vibrations produce sound waves in the air by pushing and pulling it to produce pressure changes. We hear the sound when these waves reach our ears. There is no sound on the moon because there is no air to carry the waves.

BEAT THE DRUM

1. Stretch a piece of thick polyethylene or plastic over the open top of a pail or large can. A metal pail will be more effective than a plastic one.

2. Keep the plastic in place with string, or with rubber bands. Pull the polyethylene down to make a tight skin and trim the spare polyethylene away.

3. To give your drum a professional finished look, make a cardboard cover to decorate the outside of it. Make the cover 0.5in taller than your drum and leave 5 in overlap for attaching it on when it is finished.

4. A rectangle of white cardboard is ideal for the cover. Work out a pattern using other colors of cardboard, or you could use scraps of material, paints, felt tip pens, wax crayons etc. The green strips shown above provide a border that gives a neat look to the whole thing.

5. Wooden drumsticks are best. Make sure they have rounded ends and finish them off with a touch of paint. Now your drum is ready to play. Remember – don't hit your drum too hard or you will quickly damage the skin.

Compressions

Vibrations

WHY IT WORKS

When you bang the top of the drum, the plastic skin vibrates. As the skin moves up, it pushes against the air and causes a compression, or squashing, of the air above the drum. As it moves down, it compresses the air below the skin, while just above it the air expands to fill the space. As the skin vibrates and moves up again, an expansion is caused below the skin and a new compression takes place above it. One compression and one expansion together is called one cycle. A series of cycles makes a sound wave.

BRIGHT IDEAS

Put sand or grains of rice onto your drum and bang it. Watch the vibrations of the drum's skin make the sand or rice vibrate, too. Does a loud bang make bigger vibrations?
Watch the loudspeakers in a radio or stereo. Can you see them vibrate? Is there a difference when the sound is turned louder?

SOUND WAVES

Sound waves are similar to light waves in some ways. Like a beam of light can be reflected from a mirror, so a sound can be reflected from a surface like a wall. If you shout loudly in your school hall, the sound waves travel to the wall and are bounced back, reaching your ears a split second later – this is an echo. Bats make use of echoes when finding their way, or hunting. They give out a very high pitched sound that bounces back from objects or insects, telling them how far away things are. We can also use this method to find objects that we cannot see. Sonar uses sound to locate objects at the bottom of the sea, such as shipwrecks and shoals of fish.

FIRING WAVES

1. This cannon will send a narrow "beam" of sound waves. Begin by making a pair of wheels for your cannon using circles of cardboard, paper plates, thread spools, and a wooden stick.

1

2. Make a large tube of stiff cardboard for the cannon itself, 18-20 inches in diameter, and four feet long. Make the back of the cannon by covering a circle of cardboard with plastic wrap. Fix it **2** with tape.

3

3. The front of the cannon is a disk of stiff cardboard with a 1 in hole in the center. You could decorate this with a disk of colored paper.

1

4

4. Tape the ends of the cannon firmly with double sided tape – this will enable you to fix the ends onto the tube and not into it.

5. Fix the tube to the wheels with tape, and weight the back end of the cannon so that it does not tip forward. Aim the cannon at a wall and tap the plastic wrap quite firmly – from a distance you should get an echo. Make a curtain from 0.5 in strips of foil. Fire your cannon at the curtain. You should see the sound waves making the foil vibrate.

5

WHY IT WORKS

When you strike the piece of plastic wrap (diaphragm) on the cannon, the vibrations lead to sound waves being formed. The waves travel outward from the diaphragm, making the air particles around move back and forth in the same direction. When the waves leaving the front of the cannon meet a solid object, some of them are reflected while some continue traveling through the object, making it move slightly like the air particles. A bat uses sound to find objects in the dark. It produces sounds and then listens for the echoes to be reflected. This is called echolocation.

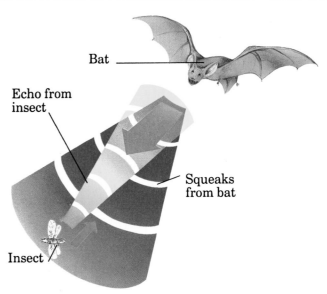

Bat

Echo from insect

Squeaks from bat

Insect

BRIGHT IDEAS

☀ Which surfaces are best for echoing? Can you make an echo in a bathroom, a kitchen, a cafeteria, a hall, a subway? Try other places, too. Do you think hard surfaces are better than soft surfaces for giving echoes? Which sounds echo the best?

☀ Try shouting, knocking two stones together, banging two blocks of wood together, whistling, and talking. Do short, sharp sounds echo better than long soft ones?

☀ The cannon channels the sound waves in one direction. Make a megaphone to channel your voice. Make a narrow cone, and then a wide cone. Shout to a friend through each cone. Shout again, aiming the megaphone 30 feet to their side. What happens? Which cone makes your voice sound louder, and which can you hear best from the side? Can you figure out why?

HOW SOUNDS ARE HEARD

When sound waves enter our ears, they strike the eardrum which vibrates back and forth. This in turn causes tiny bones called ossicles to vibrate. These vibrations are turned by our "inner ear" into electrical signals that pass along nerves to the brain. When the signals reach the brain, we hear sounds. People cannot hear some sounds because they are too high or too low – not everyone can hear the high-pitched squeak of a bat. Dogs can hear higher pitched sounds than people, and a scientist called Sir Francis Galton (1822–1911) invented a whistle for calling dogs which was too high for people to hear. This kind of sound is called ultrasonic sound, or ultrasound.

WHY IT WORKS

The sound waves from your friend's voice make the plastic wrap vibrate. These vibrations are transmitted into your cardboard "ossicles" and can be seen by watching the mirror for movements. This is a simple model of how a real ear works.

Vibrations in the air (sound waves) enter the outer ear and make the eardrum itself vibrate. The three bones, the malleus, the incus, and the stapes, together known as the ossicles, transmit the vibrations through the middle ear

to the oval window, or vestibular fenestra. The force of the vibrations on the oval window is over 20 times greater than that of the original vibrations on the eardrum. The oscillations (or vibrations) of the stapes makes the fluid in the part of the inner ear called the cochlea vibrate. The cochlea also contains fibers that pick up the vibrations and send messages along nerves to the brain. Other parts of the ear control our balance – these are called semicircular canals.

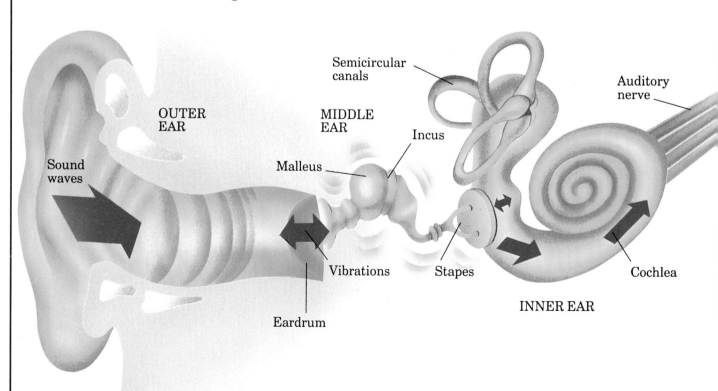

HEAR THIS?

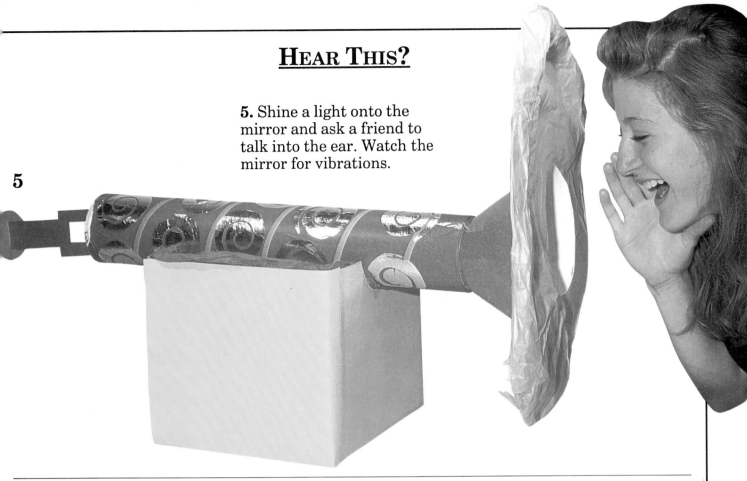

5. Shine a light onto the mirror and ask a friend to talk into the ear. Watch the mirror for vibrations.

5

1

1. To make an eardrum, stretch a piece of plastic wrap or a piece of an old balloon across the end of a tube. Fix in place with a rubber band.

3

2. Make a set of "ossicles" with two disks and a fork shape of thin cardboard held together with double sided tape.

2

3. Attach a small mirror or a disk of shiny foil to one end, and attach the other to the plastic wrap "eardrum" on the tube. Your middle ear is complete.

4. Make an outer ear from a cone of cardboard with a hole at its end. With careful use of pink tissue paper you can achieve quite a realistic look!

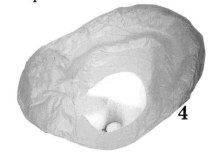

4

BRIGHT IDEAS

Watch the oval window of your ear again. How does it respond to shouting, whispering, whistling etc? The vibrations of your oval window could be a result of blowing on the eardrum, rather than the vibrations of sound waves. Use a radio to create sound without blowing.

A hundred years ago, people who suffered from hearing loss used ear trumpets. Find out about these devices! Can you make your own?

Listen to sounds blindfolded. Put your hand over one ear and try to tell which direction a sound is coming from. Listen to the same sound with both ears. Can you hear a difference? It is easier to hear the direction of sound with both ears.

TRAVELING SOUNDS

It is not only air that can transmit sound waves. North American Indians knew that the ground itself could carry sound waves, and would listen to the noises of approaching animals and enemies by putting their ears to the ground. Swimmers can hear sound through the water. Whales and dolphins can communicate underwater. Some substances are better transmitters of sound than others, and sound travels faster through some materials, for example steel, than others, like air.

BUILD A TELEPHONE

1. You can make a simple "string telephone" and see how a piece of string transmits sounds. Pierce a small hole in the bottom of a plastic cup with a sharp pencil. Repeat with a second cup.

2. Thread a piece of thin string through the cups and tie several knots in each end of the string. You can decorate your cups by painting them if you want to.

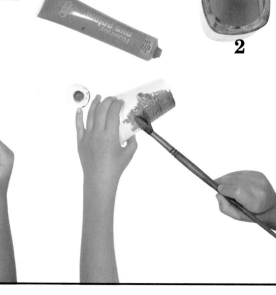

1

2

WHY IT WORKS

When you talk into the plastic cup, your voice makes sound waves that travel through the air. When the vibrations of the air reach the cup, the plastic begins to vibrate in response. Substances that carry sound are called the sound medium. When the string vibrates, it acts as a sound medium, carrying the sound waves to the other cup. Here, the vibrations cause the air inside and around the cup to oscillate, too – carrying the sound to the receiver's ear.

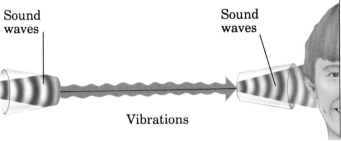

Sound waves

Sound waves

Vibrations

BRIGHT IDEAS

☀ Suspend a long, loose spring, such as a Slinky, on pieces of cotton so that it is hanging horizontally. Tap one end with a spoon. Can you see the vibrations travel along the spring? It is carrying the sound waves and acting as a sound medium.

☀ Put a glass to the wall. Put your ear to the glass. Can you hear noises in the next room? The wall and the glass are acting as sound media.

☀ Ask a friend to bang two stones together in a bucket of water. Listen to the sound through a piece of hose pipe which has one end in the water.

3. You will need a friend for the next step. Pull the cups apart so that the string is stretched quite tightly – now you can send a telephone message. If you touch the string while you are talking you will feel the vibrations – but is the message still as clear?

3

111

AMPLITUDE AND LOUDNESS

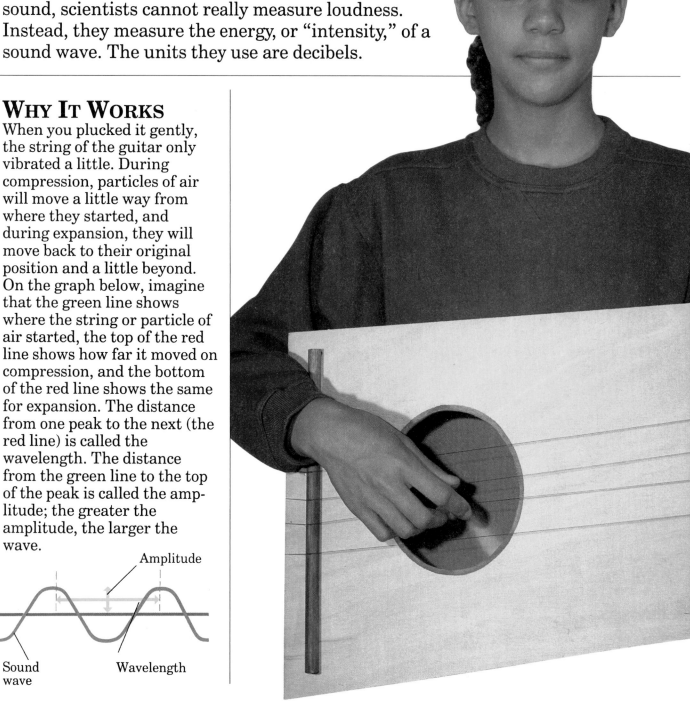

This is an oscilloscope – a machine that can measure sound waves. The louder a sound is, the higher the wave patterns will be from top to bottom. When an object vibrates, the air surrounding it moves back and forth as well (creating a sound wave – see page 104). The distance each particle of air moves from its starting position is called the amplitude of the wave. As loudness depends on a person's ability to hear a sound, scientists cannot really measure loudness. Instead, they measure the energy, or "intensity," of a sound wave. The units they use are decibels.

WHY IT WORKS

When you plucked it gently, the string of the guitar only vibrated a little. During compression, particles of air will move a little way from where they started, and during expansion, they will move back to their original position and a little beyond. On the graph below, imagine that the green line shows where the string or particle of air started, the top of the red line shows how far it moved on compression, and the bottom of the red line shows the same for expansion. The distance from one peak to the next (the red line) is called the wavelength. The distance from the green line to the top of the peak is called the amplitude; the greater the amplitude, the larger the wave.

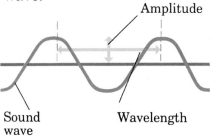

Amplitude

Sound wave

Wavelength

STRUMMING AWAY

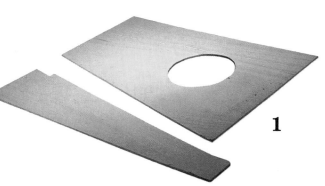

1

1. You can make your own guitar, but you will need a little help from an adult. Cut a piece of plywood 24 in by 16 in and make a wide hole 6 in from one end. Use sandpaper to remove the rough edges.

2. Ask an adult to cut two pieces of copper pipe or wood dowels, 12 in long. For the strings you can use thin wire or string, but fishing line gives the best results. Cut four or five lengths.

3. Fix the strings to metal eyes screwed into the plywood. If the ends come out on the other side, cover them with a little tape. To give a range of notes, tighten the top strings more than the bottom ones. Note where the copper pipes or wood dowels go.

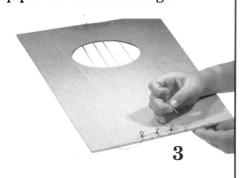

3

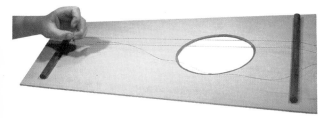

2

4

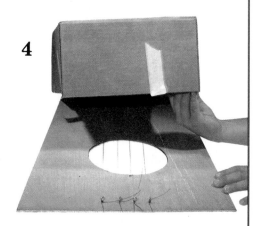

4. A soundbox made of cardboard can now be fixed to the back of your guitar. A wooden box, however, gives a better sound quality. Now you are ready to play your guitar!

BRIGHT IDEAS

☀ Remove the soundbox and listen – is the guitar as loud? Inside the soundbox, the sound waves bounce around (reverberate) before escaping through the hole.

☀ Try a larger or a smaller sound box. Does this make any difference?

☀ Ask a friend to play your guitar and listen to it first from in front, and then from behind. Is there a difference in loudness?

☀ See if you can borrow a tuning fork. Tap the tuning fork on a wooden block (not metal or stone as this will damage it). Listen to the tuning fork. Now tap the tuning fork again and gently hold its base onto different objects, for example, a cookie jar, a table, a cushion, your guitar. The hard objects reverberate more and make the sounds louder than the soft objects.

STOPPING SOUND

Do you like singing in the bath? Somehow your voice can sound more powerful, can't it? This is because the sound waves are reflected off the hard, flat surface of the bathroom walls; the sound "reverberates." In a room like your living room, your voice will sound weaker because the sound is soaked up by the drapes and the furniture. In a recording studio, the engineers have to be very careful not to have too much reverberation, but not to have too dead a sound either. They also soundproof the walls to keep the sounds in!

SOUNDPROOFING

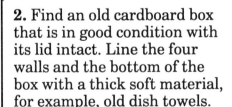

1. You can make a soundproof box to give the same effect as an insulated recording studio. Begin by collecting five or six old cardboard cartons used for storing eggs.

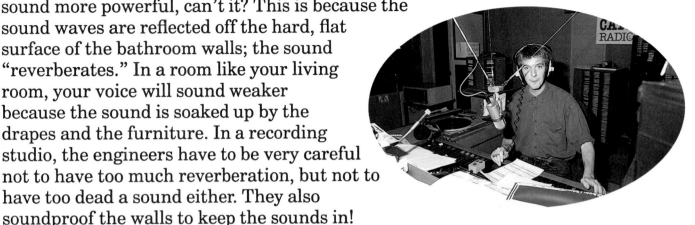

3. Cut the egg cartons carefully to size so that they fit neatly and exactly into the inside of the box. Line the bottom and all four walls with the boxes, saving one for the top.

2. Find an old cardboard box that is in good condition with its lid intact. Line the four walls and the bottom of the box with a thick soft material, for example, old dish towels.

4. When you have done this, make sure all your linings are held in securely. Next, prepare the top insulation of egg carton and cloth.

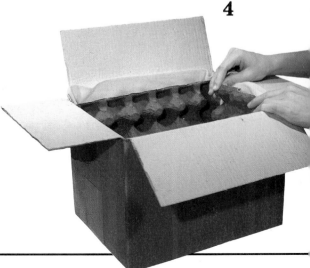

5. To test the soundproof qualities of your box you need a portable radio, or perhaps a portable alarm clock, a music box, or a toy that buzzes. Turn on your "noise-maker" and place it carefully into the box. Make sure it is something really noisy that you would normally be able to hear through the walls of a box.

5

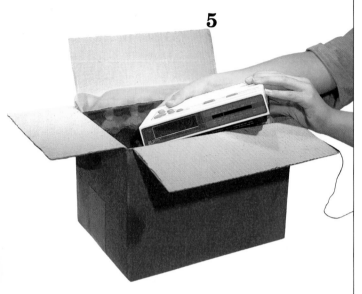

6. Insert your final layer of insulation and close the lid of the box. Notice what has happened to the level of the noise. The intensity of sound is measured in decibels. The quietest sound people can hear is about 20 decibels, and the loudest they can stand is 120 decibels. How many decibels do you think your soundproof box has cut out?

6

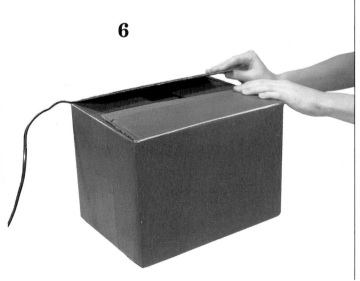

WHY IT WORKS
Your box stops the sounds of the radio in two ways. First of all, the soft materials that the egg carton and the towel are made from, are poor transmitters of sound. They do not vibrate and do not cause reverberation. Second, there are no solid, flat surfaces inside the box for sounds to echo or bounce off. Instead, the uneven surface of the egg cartons absorbs the sound, weakening it. The acoustic qualities of the box prevent the energy of the sound from escaping.

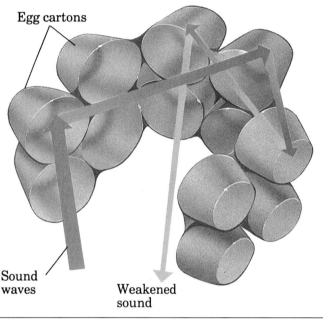

Egg cartons

Sound waves

Weakened sound

BRIGHT IDEAS
Materials that stop sounds from traveling are called insulators. Experiment with different materials to find good and bad insulators. You could try styrofoam tiles, carpet squares, newspaper, wood, and so on.

Call to someone through a window. Can they hear you? Try this again through a double glazed window – is it easy to hear? The space, or cavity, between the two panes of double glazing helps to insulate and keep out noise.

Can you make yourself some noiseproof earmuffs?

Do you have a toy that buzzes, like a wind-up train? Wind it up and let it go on a table (lay it on its side so it doesn't roll away). Listen to the noise. Now insulate it by standing it on a soft cloth or dish towel. Has the noise been lessened?

FREQUENCY

Have you ever heard an organ playing? The notes that come from the larger pipes can be very low, while the notes from the smaller pipes are much higher. The higher pitched sounds have a higher frequency. Do you remember how a sound wave is made of expansions and compressions of air? One compression and one expansion is called a cycle. An object vibrating very quickly would have more cycles in one second. Scientists measure frequency in cycles per second, or hertz. One cycle per second is one hertz. A piano string that gives a high note vibrates at about 4,000 hertz. The lowest frequency that a good human ear can hear is about 20 hertz, the highest is 20,000 hertz. Radio and other frequencies are also measured in hertz.

BOTTLE XYLOPHONE

1. You can make a simple bottle xylophone. Find five bottles that are all the same and wash them well. Color some water with a little food coloring – this will make it easier for you to see what you are doing. Put different amounts of water into the bottles, as shown below.

WHY IT WORKS

The air inside the organ pipe vibrates and produces the musical note. In a large pipe there is more air, which vibrates slowly, making a low frequency sound. The small pipes contain less air, which vibrates more quickly, and the higher frequency of the sound waves sounds higher pitched to us. Your bottle xylophone works in the same way – where there is more water and less air to vibrate, the sound waves have a higher frequency.

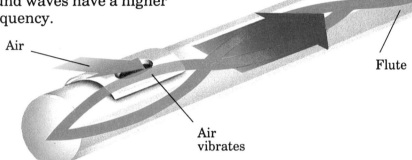

Air

Flute

Air vibrates

2. Stand the bottles on a piece of styrofoam or wool and make your musical sounds by tapping gently with a spoon or a wooden stick above the water line. To get a good range of notes you can alter the amount of water in each bottle. As an alternative, you can blow across the top of the bottle to make a sound. Can you play a tune?

2

BRIGHT IDEAS

🔆 Make some flowerpot chimes. Hang pots of different sizes and gently strike them with a wooden stick. (The pots must be clay ones, not plastic.)

🔆 Make your own set of tubular bells. You will need help from an adult here. Cut 6 lengths of copper pipe at 1.5 in, 3 in, 4.5 in and so on to 6 in. Tape a 12 in loop of string onto each one and hang them over a pole or stick. You can play the "bells" by hitting them with a spoon or stick.

🔆 Make notes with very high frequencies on your bottle xylophone. Find the highest note you can make. Do the same for low frequencies.

HIGH AND LOW PITCH

Notes with a high frequency have a high pitch, and it is the pitch of the sound, rather than the frequency, that we hear. The notes on the left-hand side of a piano have a low pitch – they are deeper sounds; those on the right are higher pitched. In a band, like a jazz band, different instruments tend to produce different ranges of pitch. A trumpet is higher pitched than a bass drum or a double bass. Notes with the same pitch can sound quite different though – a middle C from a violin is quite distinct from the same note of a piano. They do not have the same "tone quality."

PLUCK THAT BASS!

1. You can have a lot of fun playing your own version of a double bass. Here is how to make one. Start by finding a wooden pole about five feet long – an old broom handle would do. You can paint it with gloss paint.

1

2. Knot the end of a piece of strong string and attach it to the end of the wooden pole with a thumbtack or a small nail. Next you will need a large cardboard box – the bigger the better. Secure the lid down tightly and cut a hole 10 inches in diameter into the top.

2

3. Paint the box and then make a small hole in the top. Push the pole through so that the base rests on the bottom of the box. Carefully push a sharp stick or nail across the corner and loop a second piece of string around the ends, as shown on the far right.

4. Attach your string securely to the loop, and now you can play your double bass. Hold the pole and pull it away from the box to produce notes with a higher pitch. Relax your hold and slacken the string to make lower pitched sounds. Next, write your own jazz song!

3

4

WHY IT WORKS
When you pluck the string in a slack state, it vibrates more slowly and therefore its frequency is lower. The top blue line shows a slow vibration with only two cycles. The note produced would be of a low pitch. When you pull the string tight and pluck it again, it vibrates more quickly and its frequency is raised. The bottom blue line shows four cycles in the same amount of time it took the top one to complete two. This would produce a higher pitched note. In actual fact, the high-pitched note of your double bass is probably vibrating at about 250 cycles per second. Therefore it has a frequency of 250 hertz.

Slow vibration

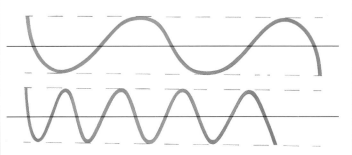

Faster vibration

BRIGHT IDEAS
☀ Try changing your double bass string for a thicker string, or fishing line, or wire. You will notice that the tone of the sound is different, although the pitch may stay the same.

☀ Turn on an electric fan and listen. At first the blades turn slowly and produce a low-pitched sound. As they speed up, the pitch gets higher. This is because the fast spinning blades vibrate at a higher frequency.

☀ Make a cookie tin guitar by stretching rubber bands around a tin that has its lid removed. You can loosen and tighten the bands to change the pitch of the sounds you make.

☀ If you have a guitar, pluck a string and then tighten and loosen the tuning keys at the same time. The pitch of the note will change as the tension of the string changes. Don't tighten the strings too much or they may break.

SPEED OF SOUND

Have you ever watched a thunderstorm? You see the flash of lightning, then wait to hear how loud the clap of thunder will be. In fact, both happen at the same time. You see the flash first, however, because light travels at 186,000 miles per second, a lot faster than sound's 1,000 feet per second. The sound of thunder travels one mile through the air in about 5 seconds – so a 10 second gap between the lightning and the thunder would mean the storm is 2 miles away. A very loud sound, like thunder, travels through air at the same speed as a soft sound, like a whisper. If the thing making the sound, like a fire engine's siren, is moving, however, the pitch of the sound appears to change. This is the Doppler effect.

WHY IT WORKS

By observing the time gap between seeing the balloon burst and hearing the bang, you have proved that sound travels more slowly than light. The Doppler effect happens because sound waves travel quite slowly through the air. As a fire engine comes toward you, the siren has a high pitch. The pitch will appear to fall as it moves past you and away. This is because the sound waves in front of the vehicle become compressed together as the fire engine follows behind. This causes a high-pitched sound. As the vehicle moves away, the sound waves become more spread out, leading to a lower pitched sound.

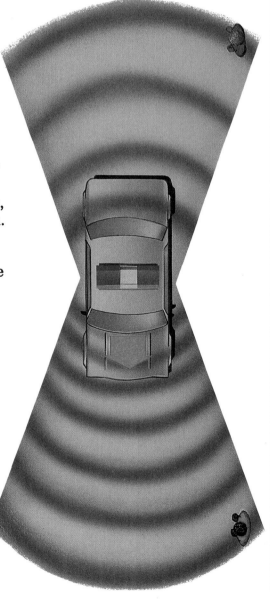

FLOUR BURST

1. Cut off the top end of a plastic bottle and fix a balloon over the spout. Secure the balloon with a rubber band.

1

2. Use the bottle as a funnel, and pour flour through it into the balloon. When the balloon is full, tie the end securely.

2

3. Hold the balloon of flour in front of you, and ask a friend to watch from about 150 feet away. The distance needs to be quite large, to distinguish between the bang and the flour burst.

4. Now take a pin and burst the balloon in one motion. Your friend should be able to see the cloud of flour before they hear the bang of the balloon bursting. This is because light travels to your eyes more quickly than sound reaches your ears.

BRIGHT IDEAS

☼ Ask your friend to stand 300 feet away from you when you burst the balloon. The time gap between the bang and the flour burst should be longer. At 150 feet it should have taken 1/7 of a second for the banging sound to arrive. At 300 ft, the sound should take 2/7 of a second to reach your friend's ears.

☼ Find out about the sound barrier. Supersonic airplanes like the Concorde break the sound barrier, causing a "sonic boom." This happens when the plane travels so fast it overtakes its own sound waves.

☼ Next time you are in a big cave or a deep valley, shout loudly and listen for your echo. Time how long it takes to return. Do you think it would take longer to come back across the valley or the cave?

CHANGING WAVELENGTHS

Have you wondered how it is that an instrument, like a flute, can produce such a large range of different notes? The flute, like a clarinet or an oboe, is made basically of one tube. By blowing across the flute, the musician sets the column of air inside the tube vibrating. By pressing the keys, the size of the air column is changed – when it is shortened it vibrates more quickly, and so has a higher frequency. Because of this, the length of the sound wave (or wavelength) is shorter and the note has a higher pitch. Do you remember the organ pipes and bottle xylophone on pages 116/117 ? Notice how those work in a similar way, as the amount of air is altered by adding water?

PANPIPES

1. For the pipes, use plastic drinking straws – the wider straws are much better than the thin ones. As an alternative, you could use plastic tubing or even hollowed out bamboo canes. You can buy these from gardening stores, as they are often used to support plants.

2. Cut the straws into 7 or 8 lengths, starting with 1 in and adding on 1 in for each pipe. Cut out two wedge shapes of corrugated cardboard (the kind used for sending packages through the mail is perfect). Arrange the straws so that the top ends that you will blow over are level with each other. Glue the straws into place making a sandwich with the cardboard. Trim the straws afterward if necessary.

3. Your panpipes will look very effective if you decorate them with paint. Glue two extra strips of cardboard along the top and bottom of the cardboard sandwich for extra strength. When you play the pipes, keep your head still and move the pipes, as you would with a harmonica.

1

2

3

WHY IT WORKS

When you blow over the pipes, you will notice how the longer ones create a lower pitch. The longer column of air vibrates more slowly when you blow across it. For a slow vibration, the gap between each compression or each expansion is longer. Look at the wave pattern at the top – the wave is a longer pattern because there are fewer cycles in a second. A shorter pipe will create a higher pitched sound, with a higher frequency and shorter waves. Wavelength is usually measured in inches from one compression (the top of the wave) to the next.

Low-pitched sound

High-pitched sound

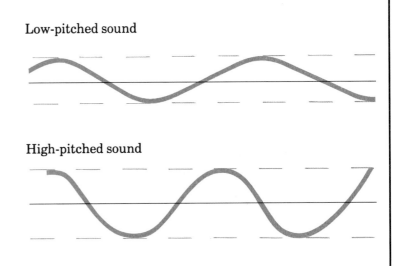

BRIGHT IDEAS

Hold a ruler flat on the edge of a table and twang it. Move the ruler out and twang it again. Listen to the sound and watch the vibrations – do you see how the shorter length vibrated more quickly and produced a higher pitched note? Twang the ruler and move it backward and forward to get an interesting effect.

When do you think a trombone makes its low-pitched sounds – when the musicians slide the tube at the end in or out? Think about when the tube will be the longest.

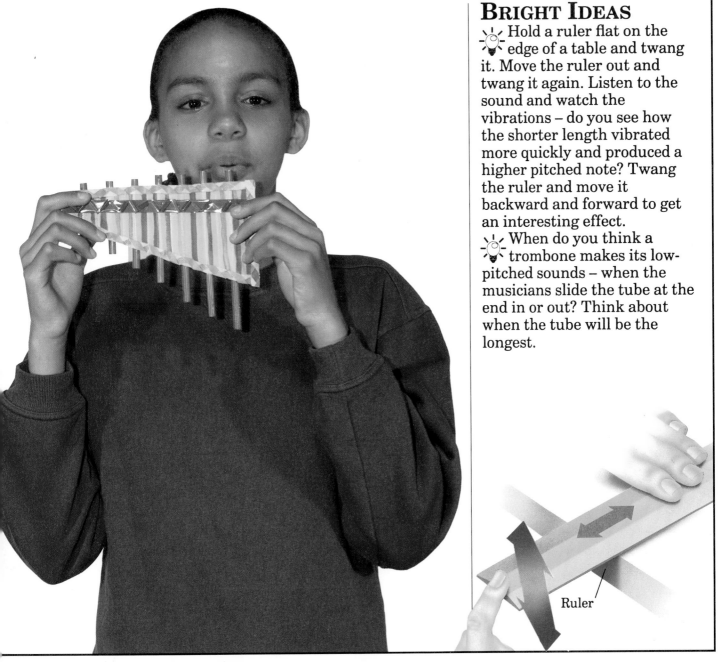

Ruler

STORING SOUNDS

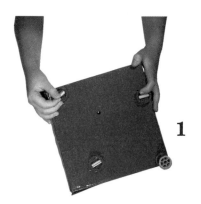

Storing sounds so that we can play them back is very big business today. It is possible to buy musical recordings on compact disks read by laser beams, on magnetic or digital audio tapes, and on vinyl records. The very first "record players" played back music recorded on wax drums, but the sounds were rather faint and very crackly by today's standards. Old-fashioned "gramophones" are easy to recognize – they have a large cone that is designed to amplify the sounds from the records. When a record is made, electrical signals cause vibrations and cut a groove in a plastic disk. When this is played back, vibrations in the stylus are converted back into the original signals, producing a sound. You can make your own simple gramophone.

SPIN A DISK

3. Make a turntable from cardboard. Once it is in the right position, push a sharpened piece of a stick into the boxtop. As you see here, the box can be decorated.

3

4. To amplify the vibrations of the needle, make a large cone from a sheet of thin cardboard or stiff paper. Start off with a semicircle shape to give a neat finished cone. Glue it securely.

4

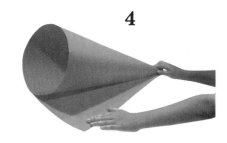

5

5. Stick the cone down to a cardboard disk and then carefully push a sharp stick through the cone and the center of the cardboard. Next push a dressmaking pin or fine needle through the end of the cone so that it faces down from the disk.

6

6. Now firmly push the stick through the spool on the corner of your box and through the top of the box. The disk should rest on the top of the spool.

1

1. Turn three identical bottle tops upside down and stick them to the top of a cardboard box as shown.

2

2. Inside the bottle tops place a small piece of plastic straw. Make sure your "bearing" sticks up and out of the top and turns freely. Position the tops carefully so that a thread spool can be attached to the corner of the box when the record is in place.

BRIGHT IDEAS

☀ Do the cone and the needle move across as you turn the record? If not, grease the top of the thread spool to reduce friction. Spin the record fast to create faster vibrations – do you notice how the pitch of the music goes higher?

☀ Experiment with larger and smaller cones.

☀ Draw the needle over other rough surfaces – what sounds do you make? WARNING!!!!!! Do not use any records that you want to play on a record player again as your home made gramophone will damage them! Use only old records.

WHY IT WORKS

Inside the grooves of the record the surface is not perfectly flat. It is designed with a special rough surface which makes the needle vibrate as it travels along the groove. The vibrations of the needle alone would produce sound waves almost too quiet to hear, but the cardboard cone and the air inside it are made to vibrate too, and this makes the sound louder – it amplifies it. The acoustic qualities of the cone would be changed if you used plastic instead of cardboard, or substituted the whole thing with a cookie tin. This is because different materials have different resonant qualities.

Stylus

Grooves in record

Vibrations

Needle

7

7. Finally, you will need to balance the cone so that it is stable – you can see a green weight in the picture doing this job. The needle should rest on the record lightly. Now turn the record by hand and listen to the music!

SCIENTIFIC TERMS

AIRFOIL A surface, like an aircraft wing, which is shaped to produce lift when air flows over or under it.
ALTERNATING CURRENT An electric current that reverses its direction around a circuit at regular intervals.
AMPLITUDE The height of a sound wave. The taller the wave, the louder the sound.
ATMOSPHERE The layer of air that surrounds the Earth.
BAROMETER An instrument that measures the changes in air pressure used to predict the weather.
BOILING POINT 212 F - The temperature at which water turns to steam.
CONDENSATION The change of a gas, such as water vapor into liquid drops
CONVECTION CURRENTS Movements of hot and cold air.
DECIBEL A unit of the measurement of sound.
DENSITY The heaviness of a substance of a particular volume.
DIRECT CURRENT An electric current that always flows in the same direction - as in a battery.
DRAG Air resistance, a force that holds back moving objects.
ECHO The reflection of a sound.
ELECTRIC CURRENT A continuous flow of electrons through a conductor - measured in amperes (amps).
ELECTROLYTE A liquid in which a chemical reaction, electrolysis, takes place when an electric current is passed through it.

ELECTRIC MOTOR A machine that uses a magnet to turn electricity into movement.
ELECTRICAL RESISTANCE The degree to which materials obstruct the flow of an electric current, measured in ohms.
ELECTROMAGNETISM The relationship between electricity and magnetism.
FRICTION A force between two objects that rub together, which slows things down.
FREQUENCY The number of sound vibrations per second, measured in hertz.
GRAVITY The pull of the Earth that gives things weight.
GYROCOMPASS A compass that points to true North because it does not use magnetism.
HYDRAULICS The technology of liquids in motion and at rest.
LIFT An upward force created by low pressure above.
LODESTONE A piece of magnetic rock.
MAGNETIC FIELD The area surrounding a magnet or an electric current that attracts and repels magnetic materials.
MAGNETIC INDUCTION Making a temporary magnet out of a magnetic material by placing it within the magnetic field of a permanent magnet.
MAGNETISM An invisible force that attracts and repels magnetic materials.
MENISCUS The curved surface of water in a tube, produced by surface tension.

MOLECULE The smallest naturally occurring particle of a substance.
OXYGEN A gas that makes up one-fifth of the air and is essential to life.
PITCH The highness or lowness of a sound, depending on the frequency of sound vibrations.
PRESSURE The force exerted on the surface of the Earth by the atmosphere due to the gravitational pull of the Earth.
RESONANCE When a sound makes another object produce a sound because it has the same frequency of vibration.
REVERBERATION The bouncing of sound waves within a small space.
SHORT CIRCUIT A broken power supply, possibly due to a faulty electrical connection, causing an electiric current to take a path of low resistance.
SOLENOID A cylindrical coil of wire that acts as a magnet when an electrical current is passed through it.
SOUND WAVES A regular pattern of pressure changes in solids, liquids, or gases.
SURFACE TENSION The molecular force of a liquid that pulls it into the smallest possible area, making water drops and forming a meniscus on a glass of water.
ULTRASOUND Sounds with a frequency of over 20,000 hertz,which are too high for people to hear.
WAVELENGTH The distance between the same point on any two waves, such as from the top of one wave to the top of the next.

INDEX

PHOTOCREDITS

All the pictures in this book have been taken
by Roger Vlitos apart from pictures on pages:
10 top left, 14 top right, 16 top right, 20 top left
24 left, 34 top left, 36 top, 46 top left and top
right, 48 top left, 50 top, 112 top, 118 top and
120 top: Spectrum Colour Library; 12 top left:
Lycoming Pratt and Witney; 14 top left, 16 top
left , 18 left and right, 32 top left and right, 42
top left, 52 top left, top right,56 top and 62

top: Eye Ubiquitous; 28 top left and top right:
Aladdin's Lamp; 26 top: the Ministry of
Defence; 40 top left: U.S. Navy Sky Photos; 44
top: C.O.I. Photos; 58 top, 92 top: Mary Evans
Picture Library; Frank Spooner Pictures; 94
top and 100 top: Science Photo Library; 22 top
right: Popperfoto; 108 top: Robert Harding
Picture Library.